# HOW TO TURN
# $100
## INTO
# $1,000,000

# HOW TO TURN $100 INTO $1,000,000

## NEWLY MINTED 2ND EDITION

by James McKenna and Jeannine Glista
with Matt Fontaine

Workman Publishing
New York

We would like to thank the following people and organizations for helping make the revision of this book possible: America's Credit Unions and the National Credit Union Foundation (NCUF) for generously funding the Biz Kid$ series and financial literacy outreach initiatives; American Public Television; WXXI-Rochester; Jamie Strayer, for her unwavering support; Steve Birge, for additional writing; Pam Whalley, from the Council for Economic Education, George Burdick, from Merrill Lynch, for content review; and our lovable agent, Jeff Herman. Last but not least, we are grateful to the entire team at Hachette Book Group and our editor extraordinaire, Riley Golberg, for her patience, wisdom, and humor in the revising of this book.

Library of Congress Cataloging-in-Publication Data is available.

ISBN 978-1-5235-2343-6

Design by Colleen AF Venable and Molly Magnell
Illustrations by Emma Cook and Noah Jodice

Workman books are available at special discounts when purchased in bulk for premiums and sales promotions as well as for fundraising or educational use. Special editions or book excerpts can also be created to specification. For details, please contact special.markets@hbgusa.com.

Workman Publishing Co., Inc.,
a subsidiary of Hachette Book Group, Inc.
1290 Avenue of the Americas
New York, NY 10104

workman.com

Distributed in Europe by Hachette Livre, 58 rue Jean Bleuzen, 92 178 Vanves Cedex, France.

Distributed in the United Kingdom by Hachette Book Group, UK, Carmelite House,
50 Victoria Embankment, London EC4Y 0DZ.

WORKMAN is a registered trademark of Workman Publishing Co., Inc.,
a subsidiary of Hachette Book Group, Inc.

Printed in China on responsibly sourced paper.
First printing February 2024

10 9 8 7 6 5 4 3 2 1

# Contents

**DISCLAIMER:** This book is for information only. We can't be responsible for any profits or losses you might experience as a result of following the advice in this book. You could do some wild thing, like invest in a Unicorn crypto coin ("But it was so cute!") and then blame us. Uh-huh. Not gonna happen. Life is full of risk. Especially when it comes to money. Be smart; save, earn, and invest wisely, and you will have a much better chance of making a million dollars.

# Introduction:
# WHY $1,000,000?

**$1** **000,000.** Has a nice ring to it, don't you think? That's a one with six zeros behind it. Eight if you count the cents: $1,000,000.00. Yet today, everybody talks about a billion dollars. That's a one with nine zeros behind it. Add two more for the pennies.

$1,000,000 can be a lot of money . . . or not a lot of money. It's all relative. To most of us, $1,000,000 is a lot of money. If you stacked up a million one-dollar bills, it would be 350 feet tall! (That's around 107 meters for you readers in most of the world.) However, $1,000,000 to a multimillionaire, or especially a billionaire? *Pffft*. Relatively speaking, that's chump change. It all comes down to perspective, and from where we sit, $1,000,000 is still a lot of money.

OK, time to get serious. Not too serious. More like medium-serious with a side of clown shoes.

Not all of you who read this book will succeed at getting $1,000,000 in your lifetime. In fact, most people will never reach that goal. If it were that easy, everybody would be a millionaire!

Saving up $1,000,000 is going to take commitment, hard work, and a little sacrifice. And in the long run, isn't that a small price to pay for your financial independence?

Believe it or not, some people would say no. In fact, a lot of people say no with their actions (or lack of actions), even if they like the idea. Many not only fail to save today's money, but they also spend tomorrow's money with credit cards and **loans** they might not need. It's easy for people to fall into the trap of trying to live beyond their means. They "live for today," but save nothing for tomorrow. But believe us, you'll want money for tomorrow.

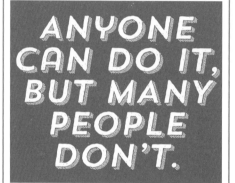

ANYONE CAN DO IT, BUT MANY PEOPLE DON'T.

# HAVING MONEY IS GOOD. WHY?

**1. FREEDOM.** Money buys freedom. Period. If you have money, you have more choices. Don't like your boss? Quit your job. Don't like the neighborhood? Move to another one. Want to travel the world? Go ahead. Feel like studying ballet? Get out your pointe shoes because you can. That's the power of money.

**2. SAFETY NET.** Life is like a friendly-looking badger with a bad temper. One moment it's all smiles and affection, the next it's biting you on the arm. Having money and an **emergency fund** are protection against the angry badgers of life. Imagine if that arm bite ended up costing you $100,000 in hospital bills. If you had $1,000,000, you could cover the cost and still have $900,000 left!

*Badgers are not your friends.*

## 3. HELPING OTHERS.

There is an old expression, "A rising tide floats all boats." You, your family, and your community can all benefit from you having money. Many millionaires, billionaires, and even thousandaires use some of their money to help not only themselves, but also others. They might create scholarships to send kids to college, donate to the arts, help the homeless, or even invest in a business. And yes, they still have money left over to spend in their old age.

# BUT WHY $1,000,000?

**W**E'RE not talking about greed here. We're talking about making money to support yourself. We're talking about **financial freedom,** versus financial constraints. A life filled with options, versus a life of **debt**. Maybe you don't think you need $1,000,000 now, but eventually you'll need some money, unless you plan on living in your parents' basement your whole life. And even then, you'll still need money.

And that's where this book comes in. We've researched and interviewed hundreds of kids over the years to learn what they've done to go from nothing to making $1,000,000 at an early age. Through these observations, we hope to

# THE BILLIONAIRE WHO SECRETLY GAVE IT ALL AWAY

Ever hear of Chuck Feeney? Neither had we. Charles Feeney was a billionaire known for his frugality. He wore a cheap watch, preferred to fly economy, and carried his stuff in plastic bags. We say he "was a billionaire" because over the years he was secretly giving away his fortune: more than $8 billion! Why? He wanted to give it to causes that were important to him. At 91, Feeney had a net worth of $2 million! Charles lived with his wife, Helga, in a rental property in San Francisco, content in knowing his incredible wealth funded many great and worthwhile causes. I guess we could say Chuck gave a lot of cheese! We'll see ourselves out. . . .

help you become one of those success stories as well.

By the way, when it comes to money, your past does not determine your future. No matter what your lot in life, no matter where you live or how you live—with a single parent, no parents, in foster care, rich, poor, urban, rural, there are plenty of examples of people from a variety of backgrounds who have found financial success. And today it is easier to get to $1,000,000 than at any other time in the history of the world. Of course, that's if you play your cards right and learn a few simple strategies like the ones we're going to share with you in this book.

And one of the first things you'll learn? The earlier you start earning and saving, the more time you'll have to grow your money.

*Spoiler Alert:* Luckily, you don't actually have to save up the entire $1,000,000 all by yourself. There's a little secret that we let you in on later in the book, where you just have to save up enough so that your money starts *making money for you.*

*Downtown before the candy store opened up . . .*

# SWEET SUCCESS

We know a 15-year-old girl who opened a candy store in an abandoned building at the main intersection of a rundown area of town.

We know! Wild notion! But totally doable. Especially if you are young. That's why you need to make the decision to start right now!

# DREAM BIG

**W**HAT would you do with $1,000,000? Would you ride a gold-plated skateboard through the streets of Beverly Hills? Buy a plane and fly to a tropical island for lunch? Host fabulous parties at your massive penthouse apartment? Well, good luck with that, because the skateboard may be doable, but the plane, tropical island, and penthouse parties are probably going to cost more than $1,000,000. So, for now, maybe your goals should start off a little more practical: you want money for a car, or college, or to buy a house one day, or to help people in need. That's all possible if you have $1,000,000. So, what are you waiting for? Go save up $1,000,000!

*. . . and downtown after!*

Her business was a success, and new businesses soon moved into buildings on either side of her. The downtown started coming back to life, anchored by her thriving candy business.

# Chapter 1:
# THINK LIKE A MILLIONAIRE

**W**HAT do real millionaires look like? Are they tall, dark, and handsome? Some. Do they jet around the world, getting spa treatments? Some. Do they drive a used car, live below their means, and stay under the radar? Most do!

Real millionaires come in all shapes and sizes. Sure, some of them may be hip, young influencers, or **brokers** on **Wall Street**, but not many. The simple truth is that millionaires are people who save money, not people who spend it.

We admit that's not as dramatic as the movie version of a superhero millionaire, but it's also awesome because it means that almost anyone can become one. Even you! Even if you've never saved a dollar in your life. You can do it if you start now!

# BUT HOW?

**T**HERE actually is something you can start doing right now, and it's as easy as putting on a pair of flip-flops: Begin working on your Million-Dollar Mindset (MDM).

Having a Million-Dollar Mindset, more than anything, is all about attitude. It means you commit to a financial goal of making a million bucks. We're not talking about a half-baked commitment. We mean you really, truly commit. Like a pinky-promise, swear-on-your-life kind of commitment. You decide that you can do this and that you are *worthy* of this. Because you are. You wouldn't play a championship soccer match without a game plan, would you? Well, just like any sport, thinking like a millionaire means you commit to a plan with goals to reach the objective. You have to put yourself in the proper mindset to win the game.

# IGNORE THE BLING AND DO YOUR OWN THING

**Y**EAH, right. Like all you have to do is *think* like a millionaire and *poof*! It happens. If it's so simple, why isn't everyone a millionaire? Temptation, my friend. The kind of temptation that is all around us. Everywhere you turn there's something to spend your money on, making it seem like as soon as you buy it, you'll be happy, healthy, popular, and beautiful, with a perfect life. It's hard to resist temptation, especially when you are being bombarded with advertisements and it seems like everyone else is buying the latest phone, game, gadget, or gizmo. You must resist, my friend. Resist that temptation to spend!

One big secret to becoming a millionaire is *not* buying the latest thing just because everyone else is. Thinking like a millionaire means you find ways to save money instead of constantly spending it. Sometimes that means holding off on the latest sneakers and maybe settling on a cheaper pair of shoes. Sometimes it means taking an extra shift at your job instead of going out with friends. It might even mean cooking ramen noodles instead of always going out for dinner.

# WAIT... THERE'S MORE!

**S**AVING more and spending less is definitely part of the MDM, but there's a little more to it than that. Having an MDM means you also have the following:

## 1. FOCUS.
Saving up $1,000,000 is a very ambitious goal. To get there you have to stay focused. You may experience setbacks along the way—jobs that don't work out, investments that lose money, and, most of all, so many tempting ways to spend money rather than save it. You must focus on ways to always be moving forward toward that ultimate destination.

## 2. PATIENCE.
We know, you want to be rich yesterday. Sure, some millionaires got that way in a flash—by winning the lottery, inheriting some money, or inventing a cool new app, but that's a very small minority. Most millionaires built their savings over a period of time. They saved, invested, and waited, protecting their nest egg (aka "investments") while continuing to add money on a regular basis and watching it grow over time.

# KNOW YOUR NEIGHBORS

Back in 1996, a researcher named Thomas Stanley decided to look into what millionaires are really like. The book he wrote is called *The Millionaire Next Door*. What he found surprised many. Most wealthy people don't drive flashy cars or take expensive vacations. Quite the opposite. They spend much less than they earn, drive used cars, and live in modest houses. They invest their money wisely—and they don't buy things to make themselves look cool. Like we said—*actual millionaires are people who save money, not people who spend it.*

## 3. INDEPENDENT MINDSET.

If you do what everybody else does, you'll be just like them, and *not* a millionaire. To save up all that cash, you need to stay independent and not give in to peer pressure. Don't be a sheep following the herd. Trying to impress people with the latest fashions and fancy cars is the fastest way to *not* become a millionaire.

## 4. KNOWLEDGE.

To become a millionaire, you'll need to understand money—how to save it, how to grow it, and how to keep it. Luckily, you can get that basic knowledge from this book! However great the advice we give here may be, it should be just the beginning of your financial learning adventure. There are so many ways to learn about money. Another great place to start is when opening that savings account at a **credit union** or **bank**. Find one with a robust website with all the fixin's. Then make an appointment with the local branch manager or customer service rep to really see what they can offer you in the way of financial information and tools for accelerating your journey to $1,000,000.

## MAKE MDM A HABIT

**THANKS** to generations of nail-biters and nose-pickers, the word *habit* has gotten a bad rap. You can, however, have good habits, and one of them would be to put away some money for yourself on a regular basis. That is one habit that almost every millionaire shares. They know how to make a mountain of money and they do it slowly, steadily, and on a regular basis.

Maybe the habit is as simple as saving a dollar a day. Too much? No worries. How about half that? What are you willing to commit to? Any amount is better than no amount. Developing good money habits takes time, but, as with anything else, you start with the first step and work your way up.

## DON'T GIVE UP!

**EVEN** the smartest millionaires can be hit with financial misfortune the likes of what occurred during the **Great Depression of the 1930s**, the **Great Recession of 2008**, and the **COVID pandemic of 2020**. Many people trying to advance their financial futures were hit hard during those times of great economic downturn. Some were able to recover. Part of that is luck. Part is perseverance.

Michael Jordan, one of the most successful basketball players of all time, said, "I can accept failure; everyone fails at something. But I can't accept not trying." Thomas Edison, when told by a reporter he had failed 10,000 times, replied "I have not failed 10,000 times—I've successfully found 10,000 ways that will not work." He failed over 50,000 times before inventing a practical alkaline battery. Millionaires don't like failing, but many of them fail anyway. They know it's just part of the game. They also know that if it happens, they learn from it and try again.

There is even a concept known as "fail faster," which acknowledges that rarely does the first attempt at anything succeed perfectly. Everyone fails, but after failure comes success so fail faster to get to success faster. Be willing to learn from your mistakes and you'll have a better chance of making money.

# YOUR MILLION-DOLLAR PLAN

**M**OST millionaires and billionaires wouldn't have achieved their big financial goals if they hadn't had a plan. In this book we will hold your hand (don't worry, not literally) through every step of creating your *own* plan to becoming financially independent. We will teach you tips and tricks to becoming a millionaire, and point out the risks along the way.

Making money is a game, and we're going to teach you the basic rules. Before we move on, we want to make sure you are willing to commit. Can you think like a millionaire thinks? Can you focus on the goal? Because if you can get into the Million-Dollar Mindset, and focus on earning and saving $1,000,000, you have a chance at making it. Start by looking at yourself confidently in the mirror and repeating the very important phrase on the next page. Go ahead, turn the page!

*Thomas "Sparky" Edison*

*Michael "Air" Jordan*

# "I WILL BECOME A MILLIONAIRE."

## LONG STORY SHORT

1. Millionaires are people who save their money, not spend it.

2. Develop an MDM (Million-Dollar Mindset) to better your chance of becoming a millionaire.

3. Don't fear failure. Fail faster, learn faster, and move on.

# REASONS TO BECOME A MILLIONAIRE

What are some reasons you want to turn $100 into $1,000,000? Write your reasons down, then post them in your locker, stick them to the mirror, tape them to the ceiling above your bed, make them the background on your phone—just put them someplace where you can see them for daily inspiration. Your reasons will help you stay motivated through thick and thin. Don't think about it too hard—for now, just imagine what you'd do with that money. Your reasons will probably change over time, so keep the original list to remember when you started your journey to financial independence.

_____

_____

_____

_____

_____

_____

_____

_____

_____

_____

# Chapter 2:
# SET FINANCIAL GOALS

FUTURE BANK

DATE 01/04/2035

10,000,000 —

PAY TO THE
ORDER OF _Me_

_Ten Million Dollars —_

_Me_

FOR _Future Earnings_

CHECKBOOK

**W**HAT kind of life do you want to live? Do you want to travel, help the less fortunate, race supercars, design clothes, navigate space, enter Fido in dog shows, or live the surfer life? All of the above?

You'll have a better chance of achieving the life you want if you have money. And that means you'll need a plan with financial goals.

A plan with financial goals will keep you from being adrift in an ocean of money. It's like charting a course for the Island of Financial Freedom. Without a plan and goals, you might

# MONEY MOMENT

When professional basketball player Candace Parker received her first paycheck from the Los Angeles Sparks, it felt like a **windfall**. She was tempted to blow it but knew that careers in the WNBA don't last forever. Players often retire early or get knocked out by injuries. So she set a long-term goal and invested her earnings into bonds (low risk) and then the stock market (higher risk). She said, "When it comes to money, you need to think through your game plan. Sometimes you need to take risks and sometimes you need to go slow and steady." Sounds like a winner!

end up on the rocks and never have enough money, particularly when you need it most.

Setting financial goals is not a one-time event. Some people have hourly, daily, weekly, monthly, quarterly, semi-yearly, yearly, 5-year, 10-year, 20-year, and even lifetime goals. For now, let's just think about setting **short-**, **medium-**, and **long-term goals**.

# SHORT-TERM GOALS
## (NOW TO 1 YEAR)

**M**AYBE you have a goal of saving enough money to go to that concert next month. That's cool. We hear the DJ slaps. Maybe you want to buy a new phone, a longboard, or supplies to start a business. Maybe you simply want to get started saving toward $1,000,000. Those probably all fall under the category of **short-term goals**.

So how do you reach your short-term goal? Figure out the cost of the goal, then divide by the amount of time you have to reach it.

Say you want some Super-Cool Thingy. The Super-Cool Thingy is $100 and you want to have it by next summer, which is 10 months away. That means you need to save $10 a month

# CHARTING A COURSE
## FOR THE ISLAND OF FINANCIAL FREEDOM

SHORT-TERM GOALS

NOW TO 1 YEAR

MEDIUM-TERM GOALS

1 TO 10 YEARS

LONG-TERM GOALS

OVER 10 YEARS

GO!

to reach your short-term goal of having enough money to buy the Super-Cool Thingy. Can you do it? If not, modify the goal a little. Either you need to get more money, spend less, or do some combination of the two. Another option would be to give yourself a little more time to save.

# MEDIUM-TERM GOALS

## (1 TO 10 YEARS)

**M**AYBE you want to buy a car, travel, pay for college, or move out of the house by the time you're 20. These are probably more **medium-term goals**. Again, figure out how much money you need to reach the goal and divide by the time you have to reach it. Let's say a trip to Europe costs $5,000 and you want to do it in three years. Divide $5,000 by 36 months and you get about $138.89 a month. Can you set a short-term goal to save $138.89 a month, toward a medium-term goal of saving $5,000 in three years? If not, then modify the goal. Maybe plan a cheaper trip, go a year later, or figure out a way to bring in more money.

*Keep your goals written somewhere that you'll see every day.*

# LONG-TERM GOALS

## (OVER 10 YEARS)

**T**HESE goals could be for 10, 20, 30, 40 years, and beyond. That may seem like a long way out, but millions of people before you have had that same thought, then suddenly realized they should have started thinking about **long-term goals** when they were 11 years old! Want to retire early,

How to Turn $100 into $1,000,000

travel the world, buy a house, have kids or just lots of dogs? Sounds like you're going to need a million dollars to reach some of those goals, so these are probably long-term and ultra-long-term goals.

Let's say you want to have a million in 40 years. Divide $1,000,000 by 40 and you'll get $25,000 per year. We know what you're thinking. "I'm just 11 years old. I'm never going to be able to save that much!" The good news is you don't have to actually save $25,000 per year for 40 years to get to $1,000,000. There's a trick we'll share later where your money starts making money for you. Don't skip ahead!

# WRITE THEM DOWN!

**I**T'S critical that your goals are clear and spell out exactly what you want. Write them down, type them up, or text them to yourself, and definitely jot them down in *Your Two-Page Plan to Become a Millionaire* on page 136 of this book. Hang it on the fridge, or post it someplace to look at every day. You're more likely to achieve your goals if they're written down and right in front of your face. And don't be afraid to revise them. They'll change over time.

# TURNING JEWELRY INTO A DIRT BIKE

Christian had a passion for dirt-biking and wanted a new bike. His goal was to buy one within a year, which meant saving $50 per month for 12 months. So Christian made jewelry and sold it to friends and family, and also set up a stand at a local pizza restaurant where he sold his products on the weekends. At first Christian's friends made fun of him . . . until he showered them in mud while ripping past them on his sweet ride!

# EPIC WIN

Jim Carrey, one of the highest paid actors of all time, has earned millions for his movies. It wasn't always that way, however. In 1985, as a struggling actor trying to make it in Hollywood, Carrey drove to the top of the Hollywood Hills. While dreaming of his future, he wrote himself a check for $10 million, dated it Thanksgiving 1995, added the notation "for acting services rendered," and carried it in his wallet from that day forth.

The rest, as they say, is history. Carrey's optimism and tenacity eventually paid off, and by 1995, after several huge box-office hits, his asking price had risen to $20 million per picture. Writing down that goal of being able to pay himself $10 million helped focus Carrey's mental state for his eventual success.

So what are you doing to get the future you want? Maybe you think your current situation is the best that's possible. Could you focus your mind into expecting success even with the obstacles you currently have? Don't wait on luck, winning the lottery, or for that rich relative to die. Decide what you want your future to be and then get busy planning it and setting goals. Maybe you need to write yourself a check and put a date on it for 20 years from now.

# MONITOR YOUR PROGRESS

**LIFE** can be like a roller coaster: What goes up must come down. Things change. Maybe you lost your job. Maybe you got a raise. Maybe that stock you invested in skyrocketed. Maybe it crashed. Even the best financial plan can hit a meltdown. Stay on top of things and check your progress on a regular basis. If you've set a short-term goal of getting that Super-Cool Thingy in a year, maybe stop and assess how you're doing every month. Maybe you'll find yourself ahead of your goals. Awesome! If not, adjust a little.

So what happens when you reach your goal? Celebrate! A little. After all, you'll now need to set a new goal and move on. You still have that $1,000,000 to aim for.

# WHAT'S THE POINT?

**ALL** of us dream of things we'd like to do in the future and what we'd like our lives to become. You will have the best chance of reaching those dreams if you set goals, write them down, and then plan on how to get there. Having a plan with a set of financial goals is the foundation for your financial future.

# LONG STORY SHORT

1. If you want to make $1,000,000, set short-, medium-, and long-term goals.

2. Write down your goals.

3. Monitor your progress, and adjust your goals if necessary.

# Chapter 3:
# MAKE A BUDGET

YOU ARE HERE

**T**HINK about trying to get to someplace new without looking up directions. Not a very smart idea, and the trip won't be easy.

Just like your map app tells you the best way to get from A to B, it can also tell you the approximate time of your arrival. A **budget** is just like that. A budget is going to help you travel from where you are now to your short-, medium-, and long-term financial goals of reaching Millionaire-land.

A budget is a tool to help you live within your means. It's a snapshot of all

# EPIC BUDGET FAIL

G'day, mate! While the Sydney Opera House is an iconic building and a global symbol of Australia, it's also seen as one of the biggest budget blunders in modern history. Construction on the project started in 1959 after the Danish architect Jørn Utzon won the Australian government's architecture competition. The project was scheduled to take four years, with a budget of AUS $7 million. It ended up taking 14 years to complete and cost AUS $102 million. That's blowing the budget almost 15 times over—crikey!

the money that comes in (**income**) and all the money that goes out (**expenses**). As the money comes and goes, you refer to your budget to see how you're doing with your spending and saving.

# BUDGET WITH AN APP

**M**AKING a budget is not really that hard. For a monthly budget, you just estimate your monthly income and compare that to your monthly expenses. Some still do it the old-fashioned way and just write everything down, but there are numerous budgeting apps readily available. They all pretty much help you estimate income and compare that to expenses. Find one that works for you, and just like

*A budget blunder down under!*

that, you're on your way! Your income may include things like an allowance, a paycheck, cash gifts, loans, or interest from savings accounts and investment **portfolios**. (More on this in the next chapter, Five Ways to Get Money.) Expenses are all the things you pay for during the month—like food, entertainment, clothes, any school supplies, and so on. List every expense you can think of and account for every single penny. That's why receipts are important. Save and enter them into your budget. Most people never do this, and simple purchases can be forgotten pretty fast.

If you find, after creating your budget, that your expenses are more than your income, there are only two things you can do:

Did we say two things? We meant three. Here's another.

Let's say you want to start off on your journey toward $1,000,000. You have a short-term goal to reach a total of $100 by saving $10 a month. With a budget, you'll know where all the money goes. You'll see your income and spending patterns, which can be tweaked and adjusted to help you reach your goal. You can even think of it as a game where you must stay within your budget to win!

*List every expense, especially those new kicks you bought, in your budget.*

# KEEP IT SIMPLE

A budget doesn't have to be complicated. Keep it simple. Don't spend more than you earn and don't forget that chunk of money you are going to put aside every month toward your goal of reaching $1,000,000.

*(Continued on page 23)*

# YOUR MONTHLY BUDGET

This is what a simple monthly budget might look like for you. Let's say last week you got an allowance payment of $20, made $40 from a quick baby-sitting gig, and—surprise—got a birthday gift from Granny for $20. That's a total of $80. Great! That's 4/5 of the way to a hundred bucks! You could even say you're 80% there! Numbers are amazing!

| YOUR MONTHLY BUDGET SEPTEMBER | | |
|---|---|---|
| INCOME | | |
| WEEK 1 | Allowance | $20 |
| | Babysitting | $40 |
| | Gift | $20 |

Anyhoo, back to your budget. Maybe you won't be making $80 each week. Maybe your income will fluctuate. Most weeks you won't get $20 from Granny. Other weeks you might sell a couple of used games or do some extra chores. Estimate your income for the next month; be conservative. Let's say you're ambitious and bring in around $170 one month.

| YOUR MONTHLY BUDGET SEPTEMBER | | |
|---|---|---|
| INCOME | | |
| WEEK 1 | Allowance | $20 |
| | Babysitting | $40 |
| | Gift | $20 |
| WEEK 2 | No Income | $0 |
| WEEK 3 | Sell Games | $50 |
| WEEK 4 | Extra Chores | $40 |
| TOTAL | $170 | |

Next, list all the expenses you think you'll have that month, including that goal of saving $10 a month. Even though your savings goals are not an expense, they should be included in the list and paid first. That's called **Pay Yourself First (PYF)**, and it's a great strategy to make sure the money intended for your savings account hits the bank before you spend it! Financial bigwigs say that you'll never make your savings goals unless you do this *first*.

After that, list things like lunch, your phone bill, new shoes, movie tickets, skateboard wheels, and paying your little sister back for the money she lent you. List every expense. It's great if you also have a receipt for the expense so you'll remember the right amount. Your expected expenses will be a little different from your actual expenses, which is why you want to review and update your budget throughout the month. Again, enter everything and don't leave anything out. If you do, you are just cheating yourself. Track your expenses each week to see how they compare to your monthly budget.

If expenses total more than income, you're going to blow your budget. Something will have to wait until you bring in more income or cut your expenses. At least now you can figure out which of those expenses is a priority. Let's say for this month the movie and new skateboard wheels will have to wait. And skip the expensive kicks and go with a cheaper pair of shoes.

| YOUR MONTHLY BUDGET SEPTEMBER | | |
|---|---|---|
| **INCOME** | | |
| WEEK 1 | Allowance | $20 |
|  | Babysitting | $40 |
|  | Gift | $20 |
| WEEK 2 | No Income | $0 |
| WEEK 3 | Sell Games | $50 |
| WEEK 4 | Extra Chores | $40 |
| TOTAL | $170 | |
| **EXPENSES** | | |
| WEEK 1 | Savings Account | $10 |
|  | Cell Phone Bill (split with parents) | $20 |
| WEEK 2 | Movie Tickets | $20 |
| WEEK 3 | Lunch | $38.03 |
|  | Skateboard Wheels | $77.42 |
| WEEK 4 | Pay Back Sister | $10 |
|  | Shoes | $110 |
| TOTAL | $285.45 | |
| TOTAL INCOME LESS TOTAL EXPENSES | - $115.45 | |
| BUDGET BLOWN! | | |

Here's what your final budget for September might look like:

# YOUR MONTHLY BUDGET
## SEPTEMBER

| INCOME | EXPECTED | | ACTUAL | |
|---|---|---|---|---|
| WEEK 1 | Allowance | $40 | Allowance | $20 |
| | Babysitting | $20 | Babysitting | $40 |
| | | | Gift | $20 |
| WEEK 2 | No Income | $0 | No Income | $0 |
| WEEK 3 | Sell Games | $40 | Sell Games | $50 |
| WEEK 4 | Extra Chores | $25 | Extra Chores | $40 |
| TOTAL | $125 | | $170 | |

| EXPENSES | EXPECTED | | ACTUAL | |
|---|---|---|---|---|
| WEEK 1 | Savings Account | $10 | Savings Account | $10 |
| | Phone Bill (split with parents) | $20 | Phone Bill (split with parents) | $20 |
| WEEK 2 | Movie Tickets | $20 | | |
| WEEK 3 | Lunch | $38.03 | Lunch | $38.03 |
| | Skateboard Wheels | $77.42 | | |
| WEEK 4 | Pay Back Sister | $10 | Pay Back Sister | $10 |
| | Shoes | $110 | Shoes | $81.77 |
| TOTAL | $285.45 | | $159.80 | |
| TOTAL INCOME LESS TOTAL EXPENSES | -$115.45 | | $10.20 | |
| | BUDGET BLOWN! | | BUDGET MADE! | |

*(Continued from page 19)*

As your budget expands, you should add a separate budget line for an emergency fund that is separate from your million-dollar fund. Some families are uncomfortable talking about money, but this might be a good time to update your parents or guardians about your financial progress and talk about the family finances. Maybe you can impress them by telling them most experts agree you should have three to six months worth of income set aside for a potential crisis.

When you're just starting off, money will be tight and you'll have to make some trade-offs. Maybe you pack a lunch rather than eating out, or hold off on the new phone, cut the clothing budget, bike instead of paying for a bus ticket, or all the above. Bam! You just saved some bucks by sticking to your budget. Now, we're not going to go all adult on you and say cut back at the coffee shop. What we are saying is you'll have to get creative and imaginative to stay within your budget.

Study and constantly adjust your budget. Work on it every day for three months and see what happens. Keep going for six months and see what it does for your financial future. Knowing how to budget will be a gift that sticks with you for the rest of your life. Maybe you get so good at it you end up making money helping others create and stick to their budgets!

# BUDGETING WITH AN APP

If you really want to be smart about budgeting, then get your hands on a smart debit card created just for teens. There are several companies who offer the card combined with an app—it's a great way for parents to load a monthly allowance on the card, and then help kids track their spending. Most cards provide the ability to set savings goals, limit spending, and donate to your favorite charity. While you get the freedom to decide how to spend, save, and share, your parents get trained up on how to use the app, which will come in handy when you need an extra $20 in case of "emergencies."

# GIVE IT A GO

**N**OW it's time for you to try it for yourself. Find a budgeting app for your phone or computer and use it. There are a lot to choose from, so do your research, ask friends and family if they have recommendations, or download a few apps and experiment with what works best for you. Budget in a journal where it can be easily updated. Or, use *Your Personal Budget Tracker*, found at the back of this book to get started. Once you start working on your budget every day, it won't be long until it becomes a habit that you do regularly and automatically. Unlike biting your nails, maintaining your budget is one habit that you won't want to quit!

# LONG STORY SHORT

1. Find a budgeting app to help you reach your financial goal.

2. If your budget is blown, you need to either increase income, decrease expenses, or do a little of both.

3. To meet your savings goals, pay yourself first!

# Chapter 4:
# FIVE WAYS TO GET MONEY

**Y**OU need money in order to make money. So, where do you get your first dollar? Well, you can simply ask somebody for $1. You see it all the time with fundraising apps, for example. You can ask for $10 and see what happens. You can ask for $100 and you may get it. What the hay, ask for a million and see what happens. Or, what doesn't happen. But let's start by setting a short-term goal of getting $100. Why? Because that's the title of this book: How to Turn $100 into $1,000,000. From $100 the long-term goal should be $1,000,000. "That's a big leap," you say. "We know," we reply. But we also know you're bright enough to get $100 and that means you're also bright enough to get $1,000,000. We believe in you and know you can do this.

# THE FIVE WAYS

**T**HERE are five ways you can reach your short-term goal and get your hands on $100.

## 1. GET AN ALLOWANCE.

Around 60% of American parents give their children an allowance. Maybe you're in that majority. Maybe you get an allowance in exchange for doing chores or as a way for you to learn about money. If so, that's great, because saving part of your allowance is an easy way to get started on the road to financial freedom.

How much of your allowance should you save? That depends on how much you're getting. Let's see now, what was our short-term goal? To save $100 in 10 months? A current rule of thumb is to pay kids $1 to $2 a week for every year of their age. So, if you are 10 years old, you might expect between $10 and $20 a week. The average allowance parents pay their kids, across all age groups, is a little under $20 per week. If that's about what you get and you saved it all, you'd have your $100 in less than two months! But again, that's if you saved all of it, which is probably not practical. If you get a bigger allowance than that, set your goal a little higher than $100. Maybe make the goal $500, or even $1,000! If you get a smaller allowance, no worries; it just might take a little longer to reach your goal.

# NO ALLOWANCE?

**A**GAIN, no worries. First thing to do is ask for one. Have you tried that? A lot of kids need to bring up the subject of an allowance. Maybe it's just a dollar to start. Maybe it doesn't have to come on a regular basis. Most of the time, it won't hurt to ask. You could make the request on your phone, but sometimes a good heartfelt note, written on a piece of paper, shows this isn't just some spur-of-the-moment idea and the request might be taken more seriously.

Here's a way to ask for an allowance that will help get results:

How to Turn $100 into $1,000,000

Dear [Fill in the Blank],

I'm starting to learn about money and how to be financially independent. I want to build my economic future and would like to start receiving a monthly allowance. An allowance will help me reach my short-term goal of saving $100 in 10 months. Please consider helping me reach that goal.

Thanks, [Your Name]

### • ASK FOR A RAISE.

Let's say you are successful in getting an allowance, or you already have an allowance, but you'd like to get a little more. Well, just as adults do with their jobs, you can ask for more money. If you just got the allowance, it might be best to wait a while to prove yourself. If you already get an allowance and want the raise, you better have a good reason ready. "Hey, Mom, can I have more money?" is not as effective as, "Hey, Mom, I'll add walking the dog to my list of chores if you'll up my allowance by $1 per week." Always ask for a reasonable amount and provide a justification for it. And again,

for better effect, we suggest writing a note along with a follow-up discussion. Everybody could sign and date it like a contract to seal the deal. You might need to add: "In exchange for my allowance, I would be willing to help out more around the house. I know you've asked me to help in the past and I didn't do my best. This time I'm serious. Believe me, I'll remember this when I'm a millionaire."

### • SAVE, SPEND, AND SHARE.

What do you do when you get your allowance? Blow it all at the mall? Well, that's just one thing you can do—spend it. But there are actually three things you can do with your allowance: save it, spend it, or share it.

Before you get your allowance, decide how much you are going to dedicate to each of these three categories, and have containers for each. Maybe it's three mason jars, three piggy banks, or three dirty socks. We don't care—as long as you put a label on each one for SAVE, SPEND, and SHARE. If you can decide ahead of time, *before* you get your allowance, how to divide up your money, then your chances of meeting your goal of saving $100 will happen in no time.

# HOW TO TALK TO YOUR PARENTS ABOUT MONEY

Some parents talk to their kids about money. But a lot of parents don't—for a long time the subject of money has been considered "taboo" (banned for being offensive or socially unacceptable). If this is your situation then don't despair—it's OK for you to take the lead on that conversation.

Maybe you want to talk to your parents about money because your goal is to start getting paid an allowance, or maybe you want to know if your family can afford to send you to college, or maybe you're frustrated that there's never enough cheese puffs in the house. Here's how to start these types of conversations:

• Soft startup: "Hey [caregivers], can we set some time aside this week to talk about money? I have some thoughts and really wanted to get your feedback." That sounds a lot better, and more inviting, than "I'm so done with never having enough cheese puffs!"

• Share your goal: This may sound like the following—"I'm thinking ahead about college and my goal is to save $5,000 to contribute toward the cost."

• Ask for support to reach that goal: How about "I don't know how much we can afford, so can we work on a plan together?"

• Budget, budget, budget: If you don't have a family budget, create one together. Some people weren't raised knowing how to handle money, or how to budget. That's OK. The good news is there's so much info available to help people run their financial lives—even organizations that will help you build a better budget. Because no matter what your goal is, it all starts with building a budget to meet that goal.

• Timing is everything: Think about approaching your caregivers when they are rested and in a good mood. Definitely not at the end of the day when everyone is tired and grouchy.

*(Continued on page 30)*

How to Turn $100 into $1,000,000

*The save, spend, and share sock system.*

Just make sure to put the money you want to save in a **bank** or **credit union** ASAP. A stinky sock is no place for your future $1,000,000. See Chapter 8 for more savings info.

Tried all that and no luck? Maybe an allowance or a raise in your allowance just doesn't work for your family's budget. Not a problem. Time to move on to a second way you can get money.

## 2. WORK FOR IT.

Another way to get money is to work for it. We know, work for money? What a wild concept.

The ways you can work for money are pretty much limited only by your imagination. And get this: You may be able to make more money in just a few hours than what your allowance pays in a month! Do you know how to

Another great reason to have a family discussion about money? After reading this book you may be able to spot a place where you can help your parents save money. Hey, it's not uncommon for adults to get into a financial bind. It happens. But opening up the conversation around money, and sharing ideas on the best way to handle money, is a great step in the right direction.

take out the trash? Feed farm animals? Vacuum a house? Paint a fence? Maybe it's time to work more. Maybe it's time to start a business. We talk a lot more about jobs and starting your own business in later chapters of this book, but here are a few tips to get you started.

- **START SMALL.** Think of extra jobs you could do around the house (most likely after your regular chores are done). You could paint that peeling garden shed. Pull up weeds in the garden. Iron your dad's underwear (easy on the starch). There are probably lots of jobs your parents would give you a few bucks to do.

- **ASK AROUND.** Ask friends and neighbors if they have any jobs you could do. Yard care, dog walking, and babysitting are classic kid jobs, but think outside the box—you can also offer to organize, paint, or sweep your way to your first $100.

In fact, working for the $100 might be faster than saving up your allowance month after month (if you get an allowance at all). Plus, it also gives you valuable skills that you can use to get work when you reach the age required in your state to get a "real" job (i.e., be legally employed). We talk more about that in Chapter 5!

*Ironing your dad's boxers might stink, but hey, it's money in the bank.*

# 3. GET A GIFT.

Remember we said you can ask for money? Did it work? Well, sometimes people will just *give* you money as a gift. Could be $50 from Grandma to $500 in graduation gifts. You should factor that money as "income" in your budget and apply some of that toward your goal of the million.

We know what you're thinking. "Does it have to be all of the money?" No. But move a good chunk of that cash into your **savings account** and tell the gift giver how you are applying some of it toward your long-term goal of saving $1,000,000. And who knows? Maybe they'll be so impressed they'll give you more next time.

Another type of gift is called an **inheritance**. Almost everyone dreams of suddenly coming into money. That rich friend or relative who unfortunately dies, but fortunately leaves you with a tidy sum of millions. You've seen the movie:

Dear So-and-So,

Your beloved uncle, Lord Sir Reginald What's-His-Name, fell from a parapet and was impaled on a crumpet fork. Our greatest condolences to you. Given that you have never heard of him, you may not feel his loss as keenly as does his cat, Mittens. As his last surviving heir, you shall inherit his castle, his collection of Ferraris, $1 billion, and one slightly bent crumpet fork. However, in order to satisfy the conditions of the will, you must swim the English Channel and take care of Mittens for the rest of her natural life. Please respond at your earliest convenience.

There's always a catch, isn't there? Also, if you get this message in an email from a "prince" and they ask you to send money back, don't.

Anytime you get a gift or an unexpected windfall it's tempting to think about all the stuff you could buy. Maybe a new phone. Maybe a car! Maybe . . . Uh-oh, we're losing you to financial fantasy! Activate financial reality!

That's why you use your budget as your anchor to keep you from financially drifting when you get an unexpected chunk of change—whether it's $10 or $100. Heck, maybe the gift is more than $100! Woo-hoo! Now, you've already reached that first short-term goal and you just got started. Put that money in a savings account today. Now. Yesterday! Then, depending on the amount of the gift, set another short-term goal of $500, $5,000, $50,000, or maybe even $500,000! Imagine if you were to inherit a whole million dollars? We'd still tell you the same thing: put it in a savings account and set a new goal of $2,000,000!

## 4. BORROW IT.

A fourth way to get money is to borrow it. A simple example would be a credit card. The card allows you to borrow money from a lender with the promise to pay it back, plus more for borrowing the money. Credit can be great, but borrowing money is tricky and, generally, a bad idea when you're just starting out. People who lend you money (the **lender**) will want something in return from you (the **borrower**). That's called **interest** (usually expressed as a percentage of the amount you borrowed). If you want to buy something big, like a house, this can be very useful. But if you want to turn $100 into $1,000,000, you might consider other options. We suggest not borrowing money until you are well educated in the ways of debt and **credit**.

## 5. EARN INTEREST ON INVESTMENTS.

This is one of the most effective ways to save up $1,000,000.

When you make an investment with a financial institution or deposit your money in a savings account, you'll be paid interest. An investment is something you purchase with the expectation it will generate income (such as interest) or go up in value in the future. When you earn interest on your investments, your money is working for you, without you having to do much but keep an eye on your investment. It's a great way for kids to make money because you can be off doing something else, like riding your bike.

And, again, you should

put that money in a savings account at a credit union or bank. Think of it as a safe, temporary parking spot for saving up your money. You will earn very little interest by keeping your money in this account, but it is a great place to build up the cash necessary to move into other investments that will pay you much higher interest, such as certificates of deposit, **stocks**, **bonds**, or a new business. The list goes on and on.

## 6. STEAL IT.

Don't do it. You can make far more money not being a criminal. Really. Many times, it costs the crook more than what they think they got away with. It is a bad return on investment and just dumb. That's why we say there are only five ways to earn money.

*This guy isn't getting a million bucks anytime soon.*

# MONEY MOMENT

Now that you know the ways to get money, let's figure out if they bring in "passive" or "active" income. "Active" income means you physically work for the money. "Passive" income is money that comes in without much work needed to generate it. You might have to put in a bunch of effort up front, but then it requires only a little bit of ongoing maintenance.

Passive income can include interest from savings, stocks, and other investments. But it can also include income from a business that can run itself most of the time, such as a vending machine, or rental income from real estate.

Maybe you become an Internet influencer and earn money from the number of followers you have or the products you endorse. We're talking passive AND active income in this case because you have to actively work to attract enough viewers to generate that passive income. Another great thing about "passive" income for kids is you can just sit in your pajamas at home and watch the cash roll in.

# RINSE AND REPEAT!

**OK,** let's say that by using the five ways to get money, you've made your short-term goal of getting $100 in your savings account. Congratulations! You're on your way to $1,000,000! All you do now is rinse and repeat. Modify your goals to go for $200, then $500, then $1,000, then $5,000, and then a major benchmark—$10,000! When you've finally got some money to work with, you can initiate a secret money-making accelerator that we'll talk about. It will blow your mind.

For now, just bask in the glow of getting to $100.

Let's check in on how you're doing:

## GOT THAT MONEY IN A SAVINGS ACCOUNT?

 Check.

## ENTER IT AS INCOME IN YOUR BUDGET?

 Check.

## STARTING TO LIKE THIS?

 Check.

# LONG STORY SHORT

*1. There are five ways to make money: allowance, work, gifts, borrowing, and interest on investments.*

*2. To earn $1,000,000, you have to start small—set a goal of getting $100 into a savings account.*

*3. Don't steal it. Ever. Making $1,000,000 is impossible if you're behind bars.*

# Chapter 5:
## GET A JOB!

**I**F your main goal is to make $1,000,000, at some point, your allowance (if you are lucky enough to get one) isn't going to make the grade, measure up, cut the mustard. You'll need a faster way to get more money to save and invest over time.

One of the fastest ways to get money is to have a job. A few lucky individuals can just fall into a job or have one handed to them. Not gonna lie— for most of us, finding a job requires a lot of work.

The good news is, now is not only a great time to get a job, but the pay opportunities, even for young people, have significantly improved. When we first wrote this book, $7.50 an hour would have been a common starting wage in America. Today, it is not uncommon to see $15 an hour or more as a starting salary. A first job is not only a great way to get money now, but it also gives you valuable experience to make *more* money in the future—even if all you learn is that you *don't* want to clean cattle cars for a living. (Our apologies to those who like to clean cattle cars for a living.) Even better news is that there are thousands of first jobs out there that you can choose from. Most will be close to cleaning cattle cars (again, our apologies)—the jobs requiring fewer skills. We're talking table wiping, taco stuffing, bathroom cleaning, roof ripping, eel wrestling, and asking if they want fries with that.

Which leads us to this: Don't be confused between a job and a **career**. Your first job probably will not be your career. There are exceptions: you could start as an intern at a gaming company and end up spending the rest of your life in the industry. But no one is going to hand you the keys to their business on the first day. You need to show that you can handle the most basic responsibilities and demonstrate follow-through to gain trust. And get

this: You need to *work hard*. A good work ethic shows employers you can handle the work. But, for now, let's focus on getting that first job.

This requires a little strategy. First, ask yourself what you are interested in doing. Making money is always first on that list, but what are you truly passionate about? What industry or business excites you?

Maybe you have dreams of being a golf pro. Get a job as a caddy or golf cart attendant at the local course. Learn cool art as an assistant at a tattoo parlor. Sweep hair at your local Megacuts salon. Hey, you and your friends probably know more ways to make money than we can list. Right? You're probably going, "Yeah, they didn't even think of *blah*. Me and my posse know more ways to make cheddar than these clowns." And you know what? You're right. We just wrote that to see if you were still reading. Ha!

OK, back to work. And that work is getting a job. So, go get one. "Wait," you say. "I'm scared." "Perfectly natural," we say. First time doing most anything can bring a lot of fear and anxiety. Try to push yourself out of your comfort zone. Just know a lot of kids have gone before you, through the portal and into the realm of gainful employment.

# "GET A JOB" MASTER PLAN

**H**ERE are the typical steps in finding a job—we'll cover them all in the upcoming pages:

1. Decide what job you want.

2. Find an open job.

3. Apply for the job.

4. Get an interview (or several).

5. Keep at it! Repeat steps 1 to 4 until you get hired.

# CLASSIC FIRST JOBS

These classic first jobs are often called entry-level positions, and they're just what they sound like—your "entry" into the world of money:

*Babysitter, lawn mower and landscaper, pizza delivery person, restaurant server or dishwasher, pooper scooper, rideshare driver, fast-food worker, farm worker, stocker and bagger at a grocery store, mail sorter, stable worker, mechanic's assistant, dog walker, golf caddy, house painter, lifeguard, music instructor, tutor, gym towel folder, theater concessions attendant, computer repairer, valet at a parking garage, cherry picker, asparagus harvester, cattle car cleaner, gas station cashier, car wash attendant, errand runner for the elderly, etc.*

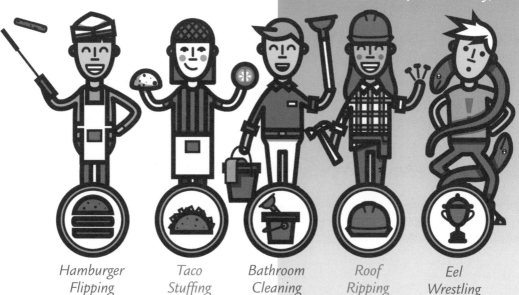

*Hamburger Flipping*    *Taco Stuffing*    *Bathroom Cleaning*    *Roof Ripping*    *Eel Wrestling*

# NINE BILLIONAIRES AND THEIR FIRST JOBS

Everyone has to start somewhere—even these billionaires. Notice how none of them had glamorous jobs to start with. They worked their way up, just like everyone else.

| BILLIONAIRE | COMPANY | FIRST JOB |
|---|---|---|
| Jeff Bezos | Founder, Amazon | Asked "Would you like fries with that?" at McDonald's |
| Oprah Winfrey | "Queen of all media," world's first Black billionaire, today worth $2.5 billion | Stocked shelves at a grocery store |
| George Lucas | Creator of Star Wars franchise | Teaching assistant for U.S. military cameraman |
| Jack Dorsey | Founder, Twitter | Created taxi dispatch software at 15 |
| Tyler Perry | Founder, Tyler Perry Studios | Wrote first play at 18 |
| Sara Blakely | Founder, Spanx | Donned mouse ears at Disney World, guiding patrons onto a ride at EPCOT Center |
| Evan Spiegel | Founder, Snapchat | Intern at Redbull |
| Warren Buffett | CEO, Berkshire Hathaway | Delivered newspapers on his bike at 13 |
| Meg Whitman | CEO of Ebay, CEO of Hewlett Packard Enterprise | Sold ads one summer for *Business Today* magazine |

## 1. DECIDE WHAT JOB YOU WANT.

## WHEN CAN I START?

One of the first things you should do is put together a list of potential jobs that you can do. Brain surgery is probably out. So is running the World Bank. What can *you* do? Don't say "nothing." Everybody can do something. Everybody can bring something to the party. Go ahead, think about it for a minute. . . .

OK, time's up! Here are some ways to figure out which jobs might be right for you:

As a general rule, 14 years of age is the minimum age for employment in America, but most **state labor laws** require you to be 15 or 16 years old. There are also limits to the number of hours you can work and rules that may prevent you from doing certain jobs until you are 18 or older. These include jobs that are hazardous—like running a nuclear power plant, operating chain saws, or driving a taxicab.

*(Continued on page 40)*

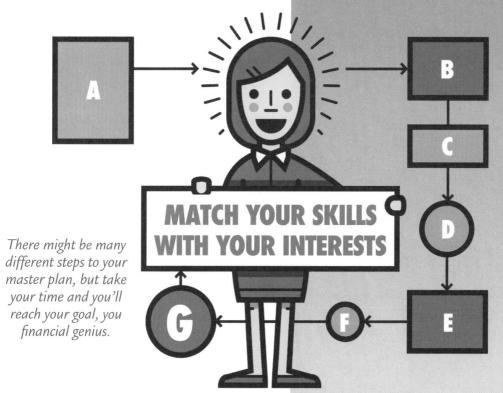

*There might be many different steps to your master plan, but take your time and you'll reach your goal, you financial genius.*

MATCH YOUR SKILLS WITH YOUR INTERESTS

It's pretty easy to look up the laws for your state online, and most employers have this info as well. There are exceptions to the rules. For example, you might be able to work for your parents in a family-run business.

# NOT MINIMUM AGE YET?

You can always work for a friend or a neighbor, if you can agree on a job and an hourly rate. Maybe you let the dog out every day for a family next door. Maybe you rake leaves for people on the block. Maybe you detail cars. We know a young kid who was too young for regular employment, so she started her own dog-walking business. If being a young business tycoon is something you find appealing, you can learn how to start your own business in Chapter 7.

- **DIVIDE A PIECE OF PAPER IN HALF.** List your skills and strengths on one side. Beside that, list your interests. What kind of jobs play to both? Do you enjoy interacting with people? Retail or food service could be a great choice. Love animals? Look into pet sitting or assisting at a veterinary hospital.

- **ASK AROUND.** Talk to family and friends. What kind of work did they do when they were young? You might be surprised at the answers ("You handled pack mules for the Forest Service in the summer before you went to college, Grandpa?"), and they may think of a job you never thought of.

- **VOLUNTEER.** Helping out at different types of charitable organizations is a great way to gain skills, try new jobs, and see what fits your interests.

- **CONSIDER YOUR NATURAL ABILITIES.** Are you an early riser or a night owl? Funny or serious? Always on time or constantly running behind? Think about jobs that might suit your personality best.

There are also **internships** offered at thousands of companies across the country. Internships usually are unpaid positions, but in exchange you get great work experience and get your foot in the door at some pretty amazing businesses.

## 2. FIND AN OPEN JOB.

The next step is to find a job that's available. There are several places to find open jobs.

- **FAMILY & FRIENDS.** Talking to the folks you know is *the* best place to start. So get the word out! Tell everyone you know that you're looking for work. Definitely talk to people who work at places you like and find out if they hire young people. You'll have a built-in recommendation!

- **JOB LISTINGS.** Search job posting sites in your area, and you'll get lots of results in a fifth of a second. Never go to an interview without having researched your potential employer—it's best to bring a trusted adult with you.

- **JUST WALK IN.** At many restaurants and retailers, you can just walk in and ask for a job application.

- **BUSINESS WEBSITE.** If you want to work for a specific company, you can see if they have an application on their website. This is especially common with fast-food chains and retailers.

*Are you a pet person? Volunteer at a shelter or animal hospital.*

# 3. APPLY FOR THE JOB.

Once you find an open job, you'll have to fill out an application, provide a résumé, or both.

Here's some information you should have with you when you're going to apply for a job, in case you have to complete an application form on the spot:

- **PERSONAL INFO,** including your Social Security number, address, and contact info.

- **OTHER JOBS YOU HAVE HAD,** including any past responsibilities, dates of employment, and past employer contact info. You can include volunteer work here, too.

- **REFERENCES,** meaning people the employer can call to find out if you are trustworthy. The best **references** are former employers, but you can also use coaches, teachers, or other adults who know you well. Avoid using friends or family members. Employers don't want a reference from your mom.

# MAKE A RÉSUMÉ!

Let's say you want a job as a barista or a grocery store bagger. The hiring manager will want to know about your work history. A **résumé** is a brief story of your work or business experience—an advertisement for why someone should hire you. Even if you don't need one for the jobs you're applying for, it's a great exercise to put one together.

Make sure your résumé looks professional. Also, you don't have to give the same résumé to every employer. You can tweak it for different jobs.

# WHAT'S IN A GOOD RÉSUMÉ?

• **NAME & CONTACT INFORMATION.** Put your name, mailing address, phone number, and email address at the top of the page. Make sure your email address isn't immature or offensive—if yours is partydude@lazymail.com, you might want to get a new one just for job applications.

• **OBJECTIVE.** This tells the employer what kind of job you are looking for. Don't be afraid to advertise your skills here a little. You can just put it in your own words, like this:

> OBJECTIVE:
> Seeking employment in the food service industry to demonstrate superior people skills.

You can change the objective to reflect who's reading your résumé. If it's a golf course, for example, change the objective to say something like "seeking employment in the golf industry."

• **EDUCATION.** List the name of your current school or any other relevant classes you've taken, including the dates of enrollment. For example, if you are applying to work in day care, you could mention babysitting classes. If you are trying to get a job in a music store, make sure you list band class. Also include any awards of recognition or the honor roll.

• **WORK EXPERIENCE.** You probably have more experience than you think. List any paid, unpaid, or volunteer experience. Let's say you are applying at a landscaping business—maybe you list experience mowing neighbors' yards or caring for plants. When listing your experience, make sure that the most applicable experience is listed first.

• **OTHER SKILLS.** These are additional skills that make you a good candidate for the job. It could include specific computer knowledge or skills acquired through volunteer jobs. If you are applying at a grocery store, maybe you have experience volunteering at a food bank stocking shelves. If you are applying to be a lifeguard or babysitter, and have CPR training, list it.

You might also include points like hard worker, self-motivated, or good with people.

• **HOBBIES & INTERESTS.** This is not the most important part of a résumé, but an employer is always curious about your interests. It can be a great point of connection during the interview. Do your friends ask you to fix their computers? Mention that here. Don't forget club memberships, extracurricular awards, or scholarships.

• **REFERENCES.** Many potential employers ask for references. You can either list them on your résumé or write "References available on request." It is very important to check with your references in advance to make sure it's OK for employers to contact them.

# CHECK YOUR WORK!

• **PROOFREAD.** Once you have written your résumé, make sure there are no spelling mistakes or grammatical errors. One mistake can make the difference between getting the job or losing it.

• **SIMPLIFY.** Avoid freaky fonts or wild colors. Keep it simple and spend your energy on what the résumé actually says.

• **UPDATE.** Rarely are résumés perfect on the very first pass. They should constantly be tweaked, added to, and adjusted.

• **NEVER LIE.** *Never!* If you don't have any relevant experience, don't make it up!

## 4. GET AN INTERVIEW.

You wouldn't hire somebody without getting to know them a little better, would you? Neither would anyone else. So if you want the job, you should know how to ace an interview. Everybody is nervous during a **job interview**. Everybody! But you can be less nervous if you are prepared.

Here are a few interview tips:

• **DO HOMEWORK.** Research the business. Find out all you can about what goods or services it provides. That will make it easier to talk about what value you can add, and how you'll be a great employee.

How to Turn $100 into $1,000,000

# SAMPLE RÉSUMÉ

The actual format of a résumé isn't set in stone. We've given you a guide. Now it's time to make it your own. Here is a sample résumé to get you started.

## Ellie McKenna

421 Eastern Road, Ardsley, NY 10530 • Cell: 444.444.4444 • ellie@youremail.com

### OBJECTIVE

Interested in a paid summer day camp position working up to 15 hours per week.

### EDUCATION

*Central Ardsley School—Ardsley, NY*　　　　　(write dates of attendance here)
**Activities:**　　Band and Stage Crew
**Awards:**　　Honor Roll

### SPECIAL SKILLS and INTERESTS

* Love to work with children
* Can create attractive posters and flyers using graphic software
* Good with Microsoft Word, Excel, and PowerPoint
* Manage family recycling assignments
* Play bass guitar
* Enjoy reading plays and the biographies of famous people

### VOLUNTEER and COMMUNITY SERVICE

**Bainbridge Hospital, Ardsley, NY**
*Pediatric Ward Volunteer*　　　　　(write dates here)
　* Occupied children by reading books and playing games
　* Made sure the play area was neat and toys were put away after use
　* Ran errands or completed assignments for staff

**Ardsley Recreation Department, City of Ardsley, NY**
*Volunteer Day Camp Counselor in Training*　　　　　(write dates here)
　* Led arts, crafts, sports, games, camping, and hobby workshops for groups of five- to eight-year-olds
　* Made sure campers were dropped off and picked up safely

### GOALS

* Plan to study psychology or music as a major in college
* Join the Pep Squad next year

And remember, with many employers you can submit a résumé even if they don't have open positions at the moment. Many keep résumés on file and call promising candidates when jobs open up. So apply early and follow up often!

- **PRACTICE.** Go online and research common interview questions and answers. Then do a practice interview with a friend or relative. Have this person ask you five or six sample questions. Learn to confidently answer in short, articulate sentences.

- **BE CURIOUS.** During the interview, ask questions about the company. What products or services would they like to offer in the future that they do not offer now? Ask where they see themselves in five years. It may seem a bit awkward, but they will be impressed. It means you're interested in helping make their company a success.

- **BE CONFIDENT.** Look the interviewer in the eye. Even if you're nervous, act like you're not! Answer questions honestly, but be brief. You don't want to say just yes or no, but you also don't want to go on and on about your trip through the Canadian Rockies.

## DRESS FOR SUCCESS

Want to score that first gig? The clothes you wear to school or the mall aren't likely to cut it in an interview. Toss the gum, keep good eye contact, and relax. If you remember that first impressions count, you'll be able to count on that first paycheck!

Clean, well-groomed hair and no hats

Avoid large and too much jewelry

T-shirts not appropriate for most jobs

Avoid jeans or too-short skirts

Dress for success from head to toe, so no flip-flops, sneakers, or combat boots

*Yes!*     *No!*     *No!*     *Yes!*

- **FOLLOW UP!** After the interview, send a nice thank-you e-mail to the interviewer. If you really want to impress them, send a handwritten note. And don't be afraid to follow up in a week or two. Here's a sample note:

Ms. Jones,

Thank you for taking the time to meet with me regarding the position of Summer Production Assistant. By hiring me, Financial Films will get a passionate, hardworking employee. I believe my skills would be a valuable asset to the company. If you need more information, please don't hesitate to let me know. I look forward to hearing from you soon.

Sincerely,

Marshawn

# EPIC WIN
# EPIC FAIL
# EPIC WIN

Losing your job is not the end of the world—in fact, it could mean a new beginning. Case in point, Steve Jobs created Apple Computers when he was just 20 years old. Ten years later, Jobs was forced out of his own company by the board of directors. After his exit, Jobs founded NeXT, which ended up developing the software used for Mac OS X, 10 years down the road. Jobs also launched Pixar, which went on to produce many animated box-office hits, like *Toy Story*, *Finding Nemo*, *Inside Out*, and more. Then, 12 years after his departure from Apple, Jobs returned to become CEO and helped reinvent and reinvigorate the company.

# WALKING UP AND APPLYING FOR A JOB

Sometimes it is as easy as just walking into your local golf course, movie theater, or burger joint and asking if they're hiring or taking applications. We know, you absolutely HATE hearing that advice. But it still happens every single day. Every. Single. Day.

Dick's Drive-In is a small fast-food chain in Seattle. They are known for paying their starting employees more than the national hamburger chains. They also offer other benefits, like money for college, health insurance, childcare, paid vacation, and incentive bonuses. And get this, you can walk right up and ask for an application. Former workers talk about how future employers like seeing Dick's Drive-In on a résumé because it means they learned how to work hard in a team environment. And almost all the employees walked up and filled out an application.

## 5. KEEP AT IT!

If you don't get the job—don't despair. Most people who are looking for work apply to several places before they get hired. The secret is to keep at it. Sometimes it's good to get feedback on why you didn't get the job. Don't hesitate to follow up and find out how you could do better, where you did well, or where you fell short. Sharpen up your skills. Polish your résumé. Be persistent and someone will eventually say, "Congratulations, you got the job."

## NOW WHAT? KEEPING THE JOB YOU HAVE.

ONCE you start a new job, you have to prove that you're worth keeping. Here are a few tips to help you stand out in a good way:

- **LOOK SMART.** Looking sharp shows you take your work seriously. If you wear a uniform, make sure it's clean. If there's a dress code, follow it.

- **BE ON TIME.** They're paying you for your time and they expect to get it! Arrive early and you'll definitely get noticed.

- **LISTEN, WATCH & LEARN.** Pay attention to people who have been doing the job longer than you have—they can provide valuable information.

- **GET INTO IT.** Find ways to improve your skills, help out when you have extra time, and put a little elbow grease into everything you do.

- **SPEAK UP.** After a while, you'll probably have good ideas for how to make things work better. Don't be afraid to share them.

- **BE HONEST.** A lot of companies have tools, supplies, products, and equipment that may be tempting to "borrow." Don't even think about it.

- **TAKE THE LEAD.** Your boss will definitely notice if you volunteer first for any project assignment.

- **CHECK IN.** Don't be afraid to ask your boss how you're doing and how you might improve.

| | | | | 2400 |
|---|---|---|---|---|
| | January 3 | | | |
| PAY TO THE ORDER OF | HARDWORKING KID | | $ | 100.00 |
| ONE HUNDRED DOLLARS - | | | DOLLARS | |
| FOR | PAYCHECK | | *Boss* | |
| 12345678 | 678910111213 | 2400 | | |

*Getting your first paycheck will make you feel like a million bucks—even if you're only making $100!*

# YOU'RE ON YOUR WAY!

**S**o you have the job, and you have some income. Congratulations! Hopefully your new gig is a great fit and you can't wait to start bagging those groceries, mowing those lawns, or flipping those burgers. Check back with your plan, goals, and budget to start saving as much of that money as you can.

A lot of employers offer **direct deposit** of your paycheck into a bank account. Do it! Getting that first paycheck will make you feel rich, and you'll be tempted to spend it all. Your savings account is just a little way to help you manage your money, instead of blowing everything. Hey, you worked for it. Don't just burn through it. Keeping that money safely tucked away will bring you even greater confidence as you make your journey toward your $1,000,000 destination. Bon voyage!

## LONG STORY SHORT

. . . . . . . . . . . . . . . . . . . . . . . . . . . . . . . . .

*1. Getting a job is the fastest way to earn cash toward your million-dollar goal.*

*2. Figure out what kind of job you want, find an open position, write a résumé, apply, and prepare for an interview.*

*3. Once you get the job, kick butt and lock away part of your paycheck in a savings account.*

# Chapter 6:
# THE BRAND OF YOU

**T**ODAY, you'll find yourself building a career and making money in a work environment that has evolved more in the last five years than in the last fifty. For one thing, you don't need to stay planted in one place, work a 9-to-5 schedule, or climb a corporate ladder. Don't get us wrong— there are certainly benefits to working in the corporate world—but many people enjoy the flexibility and independence that come from working in noncorporate places.

For many, remote work is now feasible. Imagine living on a boat in Antigua, taking requests from clients, running multiple projects, all while buying and selling stocks as a side hustle. Thinking even bigger, maybe your dance moves launch you to fame and fortune as a mega big-time influencer. There are literally thousands of kids commenting, reviewing, selling, merchandising, singing, dancing, modeling, and partnering their brand with other brands to become online money-making machines!

Today, you can design your life around what you're passionate about. Yes, you can! Seriously! It's called The Brand of You©. In the same way Nike is a brand, think of yourself as a brand. That means you're in business for you, selling yourself and your skills no matter if it's your main job, or just an occasional project you pick up in the "gig economy"—the world of short-term "gigs," where companies hire you as a contractor, or freelancer, to complete a single task or project.

The Brand of You can be fun but don't kid yourself, kid—you still have to put in the hard work. You're in charge of your own time and responsible for your own income. You have a lot of freedom, but it comes with a lot of responsibility, too. Fortunately, if you have a phone, you already have the tech you need to run your life and stay organized. Use that thing to promote your brand! The Brand of You opens up a world of possibilities to make income from a variety of sources.

# SIDE HUSTLES

S**IDE** hustles are ways to make income outside of your main job. Let's say, for example, your main job is to get through ninth grade. That can be quite an important job in itself. But getting through ninth grade doesn't bring in extra cash, so maybe you have a part-time job working as a nanny, plus you sell collectable gaming cards on the side. Maybe you also get paid to try out games and take surveys on your phone, or to tutor the kid next door. Sometimes side hustles can turn into larger business endeavors, especially when you build a reputation and gain a following for offering a great product and superb customer service. Many times, people turn their passions into a side hustle and before they know it, they can quit their day job because the demand for their side hustle has exploded. Got a passion? Think you can turn it into money? We'll bet you already have something in mind.

# INFLUENCER MARKETING

**T**IME to think big. Anyone who's active online knows what a social media influencer is. Not much of a techie? OK, we'll tell you: someone who can influence an audience to buy a product or service simply by recommending it on their social media channels.

Influencer marketing has become a multimillion-dollar industry. Today it's not that hard to find a kid influencer making over $20 million a year! (And all we're suggesting is to set a goal for *one* million!)

But, realistically, not all kids are going to be making that kind of money as an influencer. It definitely doesn't happen immediately. It can take a lot of patient trial and error, plus help from parents, guardians, friends, and even employees. You also need time to

## ETSY GIRL

LeiLei started making basic knotted friendship bracelets with friends in seventh grade. A few years later, she leveled up to crafting wire jewelry and opened an online store on Etsy called Designed By Lei. Her simple wire necklaces, rings, and earrings proved to be a hit. By the time LeiLei was a freshman at the University of Virginia she had already earned over $200,000! What started out as a side hustle ended up paying for college.

gain followers, build an audience, and find advertisers, all to *maybe* become big enough to reach the influencer stratosphere. For many, it doesn't matter how long it takes because it's something they're passionate about. If you think this is something for you, pick a dance, pick a song, pick a guitar, we don't care. What we do care about is you creating content and hitting

RECORD. We might sound like a broken record, but again, go back to what you're passionate about and talk about that. Your interest in the subject will keep your fire lit.

# WORKING IN THE GIG ECONOMY

**T**HEN there's the whole "gig economy"—those short-term tasks or projects we mentioned earlier. For those who are commitment-phobic, this kind of work might be perfect. You don't have to settle for just one company—you get to work for a variety of companies doing a variety of projects.

Think writing, editing, graphic design, music composition, computer coding, photography, digital marketing . . . and that's just scratching the surface of the phone screen.

The cons to freelance work? Well, you don't get benefits like health insurance or 401(k) matching, and it may not provide a steady stream of income. If stability is what you're looking for, then full-time freelance work might not be for you.

But if short-term contracts where you get to put your best skills forward sound like something for you, start by checking out freelance job-matching sites, or start working your personal connections to see if someone you know needs a hand.

Whether you're a ninth grader just trying to get through high school or a sixth grader just starting to think about your financial future, the Brand of You can help you reach your goals.

# KEEPING IT PROFESSIONAL

**B**E it climbing the corporate ladder, side hustling, Internet influencing, or freelancing in the gig economy, you still want to maintain a top-tier professional look. Here are some tips on how to do the Brand of You:

• **Look like a pro online:** Instagram, TikTok, YouTube—whatever the platform, make sure you have a professional online image. If you can, maybe hire a designer to create a logo (or create one yourself!). If your social media presence says you're immature or unprofessional, your chances of landing a winning gig are slim to none. You can play the nontraditional image to your financial advantage, but you can also cross a line that hurts rather than helps your image. Sometimes what was hip or funny before isn't so hip or funny now, so be careful what you post and how you present yourself online.

• **Eliminate distractions:** Focus. Find a separate quiet space to work. If your house is too distracting because Fido is barking, the washing machine is spinning, and your little sister is practicing for her piano recital, head to the library. You could also try a coffee shop, community center, or friend's house. Just make sure it is a safe place that works for you. Sometimes, a new environment to work in is just what you need to be inspired for your next big idea.

• **Get organized:** Time to get hyper-organized and efficient. Do your best to get a system in place to manage your work: a decent phone, laptop, calendar, speakers, headset, client tracker, accounting software. . . . Whoa, stop right there! It doesn't have to cost a fortune to get started. Maybe just start with a decent phone and savings and check-

ing accounts. As you grow, you can add what you need to help things run smoothly.

• **Deliver on time, on budget:** And maybe add a little something extra. It might sound cliché, but going that extra mile will result in repeat customers. We've all seen the difference between a company that offers a great customer experience and one that doesn't. Try to be the best at what you have to offer, because that's what will make customers come to you instead of the competition.

• **Flexibility is key:** Now, more than ever, it can pay to be flexible. "Work" for you might not be a straight line; it may end up being a zigzag of serendipitous opportunities. Whether you're co-working on an animation project from your basement, mixing music files from a coffee shop, or taking client calls on the back of a donkey in the Grand Canyon, the path to success can be different for different people. One thing is for sure, flexibility is key. We don't mean contortionist flexibility. (Although you may be able to make money teaching yoga online to rich senior citizens.) We mean, as head of the Brand of You, you can do most anything you are passionate about, and do it at just about any time and from most anywhere in the world.

• **Keep learning:** "Knowledge is power." Not our quote, but the dude who said it knew what he was talking about. So, don't be afraid to crack open a book or a webpage and soak up the knowledge. Look for highly desirable skills requested by potential employers, then study up (and maybe get certified, if needed). There are so many free or cost-effective courses and tutorials online to keep you sharp and competitive. Once you develop the skills people are willing to pay for, put yourself out there in the gig economy. Do a bang-up job, get some positive testimonials and reviews, and boom, your side hustle is launched! Now you've got work in the gig economy. Who knows, maybe you'll become the next mega influencer.

# THE BRAND OF YOU IS SUCCESSFULLY SUCCESSFUL!

**W**HAT happens if your brand blows up? In a good way, we mean? Like, you start really making money. The first thing you should do is hire a bookkeeper to help you keep track of income and expenses and keep everything legit—we're talking taxes, bills, transactions, the kind of stuff you're going to need a helping hand with. One day you may want to partner with a really big company, and they'll want to know that everything was done

# THE BRAND OF
# YOU IN ACTION

## YOUTUBE STAR @MISSTIFFANYMA

Tiffany Ma is a mega YouTube star with over 2 million subscribers. Even more impressive is how she's grown her personal brand by consistently re-investing money back into her business. Tiffany started her YouTube channel with an old webcam that she "stole" from her sister to make cheesy videos in high school. With her first $100 she upgraded to a better camera, and then continued to save and reinvest 50% to 75% of all earnings back into building her lifestyle YouTube channel. This savvy business move enabled her to launch her own clothing line, LIV AND JESS, and eventually to buy and flip a home in Los Angeles. While other YouTube influencers care about wearing their wealth, Tiffany cared more about building her business. Now she's on track to becoming a millionaire—all because she was smart about money.

## LEGO BOY

Imagine opening a retail store at the tender age of 10! That's exactly what Eric Vasquez did—all because he had a passion for LEGO. Connect the Brick is an 89-square-foot store in Tacoma, Washington, that sells all things LEGO, from full sets, to individual pieces, to minifigures. You never know where a business can take you! Eric started his side hustle with a table at a local farmers' market to sell and trade LEGO bricks, and expanded when an opportunity came up to rent a small space. The downside? You only need to step on a LEGO once to understand you don't walk barefoot in this business.

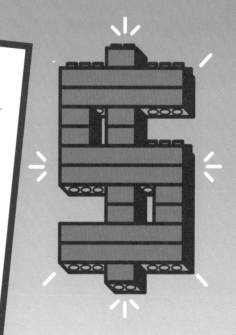

properly. And please don't hire your cousin. Keep your business life separate from your personal life!

And just remember, although the world of business and finance has changed with the invention of the smartphone, some of the old-school rules still apply. You still have to show up for the interview on time, even if it's a Zoom call. Yes, you can wear pajamas below the waist, but make sure you look like a pro above the desk. Be organized, prepared, and punctual. Follow up and follow through, do high-quality work

on time and on budget, and you'll go far as a side hustler in a gig economy.

# OFFLINE OPPORTUNITIES

**N**o phone? No laptop? No problem! The Brand of You works whether you are on- or offline. Even if you don't have access to technology, there's still money to be made. All you need is a brain and some work ethic.

Not sure where to look for offline opportunities? Ask someone older than you! Believe it or not, the Internet is a relatively new invention and plenty of people created successful side hustles without the help of technology. Reread our list of business ideas on page 67, and don't think about it too hard . . . Just try selling your product or service, and then adjust things based on customer feedback. Don't be afraid to make mistakes! Many times, that's the best path forward!

# LIST O' SIDE HUSTLES FOR KIDS

There are so many ways to make money, using nothing but your phone:

- Sell stock photos and videos—create an online portfolio of your best work and sell to a stock photo agency.
- Online surveys—get paid to respond to online surveys, and market research.
- Resell used sports equipment—if it's in decent condition, it's better to cash in than to collect dust.
- Resell used clothes—there's tons of websites that will gladly match your old threads with a new owner.
- Hunt for bargains at garage sales—make your bargains look pretty in a picture and you can pad your bank account by reselling for a profit.
- Tutor younger students—turn that grade A in math into a $ in your wallet.
- Become a style bundler—create curated outfits from online thrift stores, based on a customer's preferred aesthetic.

- Fulfillment by Amazon—find discounted products, set up a store on Amazon, and sell them for a profit.
- Social media support—help the older generation out by sharing tips and tricks for attracting followers.
- Review music—at $0.05 to $0.20 per song, you are not going to see a huge amount of revenue, but every bit can add up.

Side hustles that need a bit more than just a phone:

- Create a course—have skills at baking cakes? Writing code? Grooming cats? Many "subject matter experts" turn their expertise into a course and sell their knowledge. Just google "online course platforms" to get going.
- Launch a podcast—if you love hearing yourself talk maybe others will, too. Pick a theme, find a podcast platform, then get the word out. Once you have followers, you can approach like-minded companies for sponsorships.

*(Continued on page 60)*

- Print-on-demand (POD)—create original designs then upload them to a POD partner who prints your art on T-shirts, hoodies, mugs, stickers, etc., and takes care of the shipping. Easy-peasy.
- Etsy.com—set up an online storefront to sell your crafts and handmade goods.
- Start a YouTube channel—build content around something you love to do or talk about. It may take years to build a large enough audience to make money, but, hey, you're young and have nothin' but time on your hands!
- Make money on Twitch—livestream your video gaming skills, build a following, then ask for donations or sell merchandise.

No matter how you choose to make money, remember you represent The Brand of You. Work hard, be courteous and professional, and follow through on your commitments. Who knows, maybe your side hustle is so fun and lucrative it turns into your main hustle, and one day into a million dollars!

(If you are under 18, you may need the consent of your parents or guardians for some of these side hustles.)

# LONG STORY SHORT

1. There are a lot of ways to make money as The Brand of You.

2. Explore online and offline opportunities.

3. Get organized and be professional.

# Chapter 7: START A BUSINESS

**T**HINK of some rich people. I mean really rich. Like private islands rich. Caviar omelets. Yachts made of gold. How did they get that way? Did they just save their allowance? Clip coupons? Buy Florida swampland? Nope, nope, and triple nope. They started a biz (or two or three!).

Don't get us wrong—jobs are great. Your boss tells you what to do, and you don't have to risk any of your own money. You can get a regular schedule, regular paycheck, regular vacation, and regular benefits. The pro of having a regular job is depending on the regularity, but the con of having a regular job is depending on the regularity.

Nothing is regular when starting a business. Everything is totally different. You become the boss, but there's no regular paycheck, no regular schedule, and you take an irregular amount of the financial risk. So, what's the upside? Why, money, of course! Big, heaping piles of money!

Well, not *really*. But the **profit potential** from starting a successful business can be greater than almost anything else you can do. It is also a great way to lose money. There are so many things that can go wrong. However, if you *really* want to make money to save up to $1,000,000, it's something to seriously consider.

# WHY START NOW?

**E** VEN if you don't make $1,000,000 on your very first try, here are six fantastic reasons to start a business now before you get all old and wrinkly.

## 1. IT'S AWESOME. There's nothing like the feeling of taking an idea, making it real, and watching it grow.

## 2. MAKE BIG MONEY.
Running a business is one of the best methods of turning some money into more. Once you come up with a profitable idea, they used to say, "The sky's the limit." Today, if you were a rocket business, you could say, "Space is the limit," because a great idea can lead to limitless potential!

## 3. THERE'S NO TIME LIKE THE PRESENT.
Seriously. There's *no* time like being a kid. Grown-ups have all kinds of responsibilities that make it harder for them to take risks. Plus, people will think you're cute, which will help you sell them more stuff.

## 4. BE YOUR OWN BOSS.
Nobody likes being bossed around. But everyone likes *being* the boss. Of course, until you can get some employees, you'll only be bossing yourself around. Make sure to hire a sibling ASAP.

## 5. FAIL FAST. Behind every successful businessperson is a list of blunders they made on their way to the top. They would tell you there are lessons learned from those failures. Savvy people understand they will fail before finding success. A failure points you in the right direction, because now you know what not to do. When you start

# CAN KIDS REALLY START A BUSINESS?

Having your own business can be awesome, and kids do it all the time before they even have a driver's license. These young entrepreneurs all made their millions in different ways. One thing they had in common? They found a need and took action at an early age.

Ten-year-old Maddie Bradshaw wanted to decorate her school locker with pictures, but the magnets holding the pictures were BORING! So, she designed her own by gluing her picture into a soda bottle cap, and then gluing that to a magnet. The result stuck like . . . well, a magnet. Her picture-inside-a-bottle-cap magnet was an immediate sensation and requests started pouring in from the rest of the student body (Get it, "pouring," bottle cap? NVM). Using $300 of her own money, Maddie created Snap Caps! With help from her little sister Margot, and a big assist from her mom, Snap Caps grew into a national brand, selling 50,000 units per month in less than two years.

Moziah Bridges learned how to sew bow ties at just 9 years old with leftover vintage fabrics and some loving coaching from his granny. Mo took the "old-school" style to another level by extending it throughout his brand—his personal style, business cards, website, and classic old-fashioned suitcase he carried to sell bow ties from store to store. Mo eventually made it to Shark Tank, took on Daymond John as a mentor, and tied up a deal to create a line of handcrafted bow ties for the NBA! Yes, that National Basketball Association! Slam dunk!

As a 19-year-old undergrad student at Duke University, Bolun Li knew financial literacy was important but just didn't connect to the material being presented. Neither did his peers. So they created Zogo—an app that PAYS YOU to learn money lessons. That's right, you get paid to learn about money! The more you learn, the more you are rewarded with virtual pineapples, which can be converted to real gift cards, worth real money! Why pineapples? After many hours of research, lines of code, and cups of espresso, Bolun and his team realized everybody likes pineapples. So, why not? Soon, the Zogo money app was born, and Bolun picked up a new moniker—Mr. Pineapple.

Jon Koon would look through his dad's car magazines from Japan and wonder why no one in America was dressing up their cars with special parts or unique finishes. Jon took $5,000 in savings and bought parts from overseas suppliers. He partnered with a local mechanic and started souping up cars with high-end finishes, audio systems, and engine work. The business took off and became one of the main suppliers for a popular TV show, making him millions by the time he was 16.

a business at a young age, you can get any of those mistakes out of the way fast before anyone is paying attention. So get going and don't be afraid to fail faster to succeed!

**6. LOOK SMART.** Being a business owner looks great on college applications or on a résumé. It shows initiative, smarts, and responsibility.

# PLANNING MAKES PERFECT

**M**AYBE you're reading this and suddenly a thousand business ideas are bubbling through your brain. Or maybe you got distracted and are thinking about how many grilled cheese sandwiches it would take to fill up the Statue of Liberty. Either way, you need a plan– a **business plan**.

With a business plan, you can spot problems before you get started, problems that are way easier to fix now, with the "delete" key, rather than after you've invested your time and money. You wouldn't want to make 1,000 blue widgets before realizing that your customers only wanted red ones, would you?

Your business plan can be really simple to start. In fact, it can be just one page. We've provided a spectacular (if we do say so ourselves) *One-Page Business Plan* template on page 138. If you have an idea about how to start a business, this is a great way to figure out the details. If you don't have an idea, use it as a tool to inspire you. But before you skip right to it, consider these four steps:

# STEP 1: THE "BIG IDEA"

**A** strong, successful business starts with a great idea. If you already have an idea in mind, awesome. Write it down on your *One-Page Business Plan* where it says The "Big Idea."

Drawing a blank? Relax—try this: answer each prompt on the next page and you could turn those answers into moneymakers! Need more inspiration? Try an online search, ask friends and family, consider what's needed in your community—sometimes the best idea comes from a shower thought.

# THE FOUR Ds OF A GREAT BUSINESS IDEA

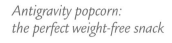

*Antigravity popcorn: the perfect weight-free snack*

**W**HEN inspiration finally strikes, how do you know what idea to pursue? Drumroll please . . .

- **DOABLE AND DIF-FERENT.** Low Earth Orbit tours and antigravity popcorn might be different, but probably not so doable. Try something simpler. Normal popcorn is doable and you can make it different with special herbs and spices, then package it in an upscale container. Call it "Space Corn."

| THINK ABOUT . . . | EXAMPLE ANSWER | EXAMPLE MONEY-MAKING IDEA | YOUR ANSWER | POSSIBLE MONEY-MAKING IDEA |
|---|---|---|---|---|
| Something you enjoy | Riding my bike | Bike tours of my town/city | | |
| Something you're really good at | Helping my parents with their computer | Computer services for the elderly | | |
| Something you care about | The environment | Helping people find green products | | |
| Something people need that they don't have now | A better backseat organizer for kids' stuff | Make one! | | |
| Someone you admire, and what that person does | My grandma, who bakes amazing pies | Sell pies based on her secret recipes | | |

- **DO PEOPLE WANT IT?** Handmade raincoats for Chihuahuas are unique, but is there a market for them? Make a sample or a drawing and share it— post it on a Chihuahua forum or ask the manager at your local pet store. If that's what Chihuahua owners have been looking for all their lives, you're set, but you won't know unless you do some research. So survey potential customers and see what they say.

- **DO YOU WANT TO DO IT?** A business will take up a big chunk of time. You'll be more successful if it's something you're passionate about. No point spending all that time building something you don't like to do.

# STEP 2: MARKETING MADNESS

**W**HETHER you sell a product or a service, without **marketing**, you're just playing store. Marketing is how you get the word out about your new business. It can range from showing the product in person and posting on social media to launching a website or pulling banners behind airplanes.

Before you can think about marketing to customers, identify who they are. Potential customers are known as your **target market**—the folks who might buy your product or service. Remember those handmade raincoats for Chihuahuas? No point targeting people who don't have a dog. Are those raincoats a luxury item? You might want to target people who have some extra cash to spare. So instead of wasting time (and money) posting flyers in apartment buildings that don't allow pets, you might want to post to community and neighborhood chat groups. Especially in more affluent, dog-friendly neighborhoods. Or throw a few dogs in raincoats on your Instagram reel and tag a few celebrities. Get the picture?

# THE FOUR Ps OF MARKETING

**O**NCE you know your target market, there are four more things to consider, and you're in luck, these all start with *P*: product, price, place, and promotion.

# EASY BUSINESS IDEAS FOR KIDS

## SERVICES

- Photograph or video skateboarders, pets, kids, events
- Gift wrapping and/or decorating for the holidays
- Babysit or parent helper
- Pet grooming, pet sitting, pet walking, pet training. You can do lots of "ings" with pets.
- Busker, street performer, spray paint artist (use those graffiti skills for profit)
- House painting, cleaning, window washing, organization
- Pressure-washing service
- Mow lawns, plow snow, rake leaves
- Errand service
- Entertain at kid's birthday parties (magician, clown, card tricks, balloon animals, game leader)
- Dance instruction
- Computer setup, service, bloatware elimination, general IT help
- Car wash and detail service
- Teach swimming lessons
- Travel, educational, or brand influencer
- Math, science, or language tutor
- Graphic artist
- Marketing and promotions for other businesses
- Organize yard or tag sales for neighbors
- Sell things for people online
- Write music, create sound effects, and sell online

## PRODUCTS

- Design and make products to sell:
  » jams, lemonade, flowers, organic juices, fruits and veggies
  » baked goods (cookies, breads, rolls, muffins)
  » candy, ice cream, pet treats, soaps and candles, holiday decorations, greeting cards, paper goods, custom picture frames, knitted hats, mittens, and scarves
  » customized decorated clothing, shoes, hats
- Buy used electronics, bikes, toys, games, graphic cards. Fix and resell them
- Write social media posts for local businesses
- Buy and strategically place a vending machine (or two)
- Make jewelry
- Sew clothes
- Bling out new sneakers or jeans

The list goes on and on. You could create a stand to sell all that stuff, or do it online, or both! Who said you only need to do one? You can sell multiple products and services! Now, get back to work on your business.

# PRODUCTS VS. SERVICES

Still not sure what business to start? No matter what business you choose, from a lemonade stand to computer repair, it will be a **product**, a **service**, or a combination of both.

## SERVICES

Services are an easy way to get started. Think yard work, babysitting, window cleaning, and more. But you're limited by the number of hours you can work in a single day unless you hire employees.

## PRODUCTS

Products are a little trickier to figure out. You'll need to sell something unique, and then find startup cash for supplies and inventory. But if your products are popular, get ready for fat stacks of cash!

## 1. PRODUCT

The actual thing you are selling your customers is known as your product (this can also be a service). Decisions you make in this category include things like: Do you have a logo or brand name? What sizes or features come with the product or service? What's the packaging? What kind of quality will you provide? Will you offer any money-back guarantees? When you think of "product," think of the whole enchilada—the entire value that you plan to offer your customers.

## 2. PRICE

What's the price of your product or service? There are a few good ways to figure out the right amount to charge:

Calculate your cost of making one unit and add a percentage for profit. Let's say you sell jam and it costs you $3.00 a jar to make. If you want to make at least a 25% profit, then you would add 25% of $3.00, which means you would price each jar at $3.75. For a car-cleaning service the cost of "making one unit" might be $20, which includes $5 for cleaning supplies, and

$15 to pay yourself (or an employee) to clean the car. If you wanted to make 25% profit you would charge $25.00.

• Research competitors and charge just above or below their price.

• Ask people what they'd be willing to pay.

• Try selling your product or service at a certain price and adjust based on the results. Doing well? You might raise the price. Not selling? Lower it.

Remember, your price is also the value you give customers. If other neighborhood kids are mowing lawns, offer to mow lawns *and* weed flower beds for the same price. If you're selling cookies, put them in a cute container. These things make your product more valuable.

# 3. PLACE

Where can your customers obtain your product or service? Will it be online or directly from you? Think about where you can find your target market, and make it convenient for them to get your stuff. If you're cleaning cars, where are the people with dirty cars? Position your product or service where possible

customers can easily get it when they want it most.

Ever notice how grocery stores put the nacho cheese dip right next to the tortilla chips? The store probably sells a lot more dip using this technique.

# 4. PROMOTION

Now it's time to get the word out. With your first business, you want maximum impact for minimum dollars. Here are seven strategies for catching customers' eyes and ears:

*Promote those puppy coats!*

# NO FUNNY BUSINESS

Let's say you, a 16-and-a-half-year-old, made at least $12,950* this year at your job stuffing tacos . . . Congratulations! You may have to file a federal tax return!

Don't try pulling that "But, I'm just a kid!" stuff on us. You might be a kid, but you still may have to pay Uncle Sam his cut (aka "taxes to the Internal Revenue Service"). Sometimes you have to pay state taxes, too. If you're not making that kind of coin, but still made over $400 as an "independent contractor" you may still have to file a tax return and pay self-employment tax. Earn less than that? Then you probably won't have to file a tax return. We say double check with a trusted adult or financial advisor to make sure you stay on Uncle Sam's good side.

*IRS tax threshold for 2023. Earn that amount or more and pay taxes. Earn less than that amount and probably do not pay taxes.

**WORD OF MOUTH.** You don't need us telling you that the first place to promote your biz is on social media. Think creatively about your posts. How do the popular brands use video and graphics for their posts? Build on those ideas and offer friends a discount to post and share. Tag celebs, do a contest, pay an influencer, and snap your way to Millionaire-land. Who knows? It could go viral!

**GO GUERRILLA.** Guerrilla marketing is unconventional, low-cost marketing techniques to generate publicity for your business. Like, you and your friends do a pop-up dance show at a high school, church, or community event. Hand out samples, postcards, and flyers. Or get an artist to create temporary art on streets and sidewalks. We know a young person who passed out napkins printed with his business information behind the flight attendant on an airplane. His story ended up in the local news. Talk about unconventional!

**LAUNCH A WEBSITE.** You and your friends may already be doing this. There was a time when getting designer sneakers ordered and delivered to Fergus County, Montana, would have been virtually impossible, or have taken months. Today—phone, done. The Internet has changed the world of business and finance. Now we buy or sell anything with a few keystrokes. Building your site is easier than ever. There are tons of free or low-cost services, and, of course, blogs are always free. No need to get too fancy—not at first. Just pick a basic template, write your pitch, upload some pics, and send the link to everyone you know.

## GET BUSINESS CARDS.

Even in today's high-tech world, the good old paper-based traditional card is still needed. Auntie will proudly hand them out to her friends. There are literally millions of different styles, cuts, and colors of business cards. You can go conservative, or artfully flamboyant. Thick or thin. Recycled! The business cards for a concert lighting company owned by a young person we know are stamped from metal.

## SCORE FREE PRESS.

Adults LOVE stories of kid entrepreneurs. You see it all the time on social media and in newspapers, magazines, and on local news and radio shows. Email the press about your business. Reach out to bloggers, vloggers, and podcasters. Make sure to mention that you're a kid entrepreneur, because you're a walking human-interest story.

# BULL UNDERWEAR

Our favorite guerilla marketing move was by GoldToe, a sock company that was expanding into undergarments. To get attention for its new products, the company thought it would be cute to put an enormous pair of men's briefs on the "Charging Bull" statue (yes, that massive statue near Wall Street). They casually placed underwear on all kinds of other statues in New York as well . . . all in the name of marketing. Now that's what you call thinking outside the box(ers).

# TRACK IT OR LOSE IT

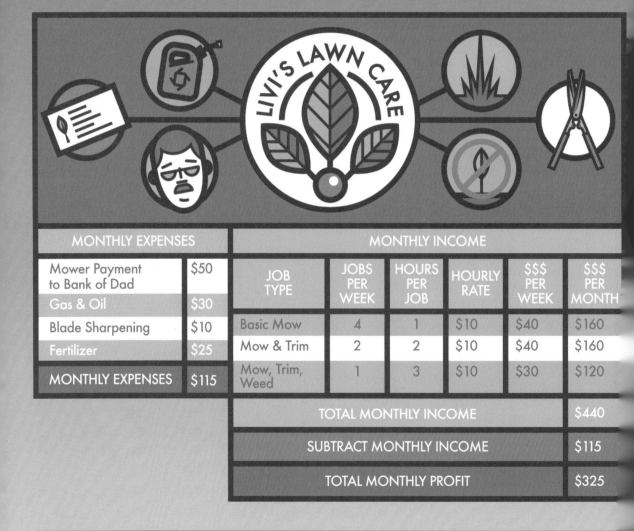

**MONTHLY EXPENSES**

| | |
|---|---|
| Mower Payment to Bank of Dad | $50 |
| Gas & Oil | $30 |
| Blade Sharpening | $10 |
| Fertilizer | $25 |
| **MONTHLY EXPENSES** | **$115** |

**MONTHLY INCOME**

| JOB TYPE | JOBS PER WEEK | HOURS PER JOB | HOURLY RATE | $$$ PER WEEK | $$$ PER MONTH |
|---|---|---|---|---|---|
| Basic Mow | 4 | 1 | $10 | $40 | $160 |
| Mow & Trim | 2 | 2 | $10 | $40 | $160 |
| Mow, Trim, Weed | 1 | 3 | $10 | $30 | $120 |
| TOTAL MONTHLY INCOME | | | | | $440 |
| SUBTRACT MONTHLY INCOME | | | | | $115 |
| TOTAL MONTHLY PROFIT | | | | | $325 |

Livi is doing pretty well. One thing she needs to consider, though, is that depending on where she lives, she might be able to run her business only in the spring and summer. She might need to invest in a rake and a snow shovel for the fall and winter.

Business is all about making a profit. Track your income and expenses in a separate budget to be sure your bank balance is headed in the right direction. You can use fancy software, or you can use a ratty spiral-bound notebook—both will do the job. Many people use online budget apps for tracking income and expenses. Just find the way that works for you.

Here are a couple of examples of budgets for small businesses.

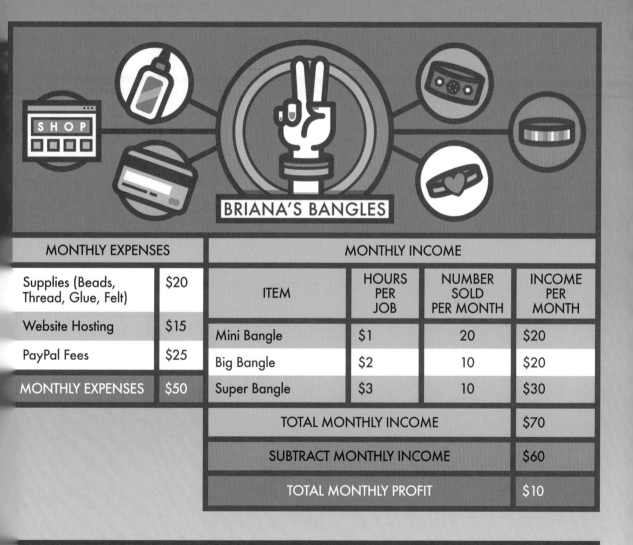

**BRIANA'S BANGLES**

| MONTHLY EXPENSES | | MONTHLY INCOME | | | |
|---|---|---|---|---|---|
| Supplies (Beads, Thread, Glue, Felt) | $20 | ITEM | HOURS PER JOB | NUMBER SOLD PER MONTH | INCOME PER MONTH |
| Website Hosting | $15 | Mini Bangle | $1 | 20 | $20 |
| PayPal Fees | $25 | Big Bangle | $2 | 10 | $20 |
| MONTHLY EXPENSES | $50 | Super Bangle | $3 | 10 | $30 |
| | | TOTAL MONTHLY INCOME | | | $70 |
| | | SUBTRACT MONTHLY INCOME | | | $60 |
| | | TOTAL MONTHLY PROFIT | | | $10 |

Briana's only making $10 a month in profit! She needs to step up her marketing, cut her costs, or improve her products to increase sales. Luckily, because she was tracking her income and expenses, she can fix things fast.

# WHERE TO FIND FUNDING

So . . . you got a great idea, great plan, and great potential to make great profit. Only catch is you need money to start your business. Let's say it's a car-detailing business, and costs $1,500 to start up. But you only have $500 in savings. What do you do?

• **Bootstrap it**—Entrepreneurs "bootstrap" their businesses all the time. To bootstrap means you beg and borrow (but not steal) your way forward, to keep expenses as low as possible and get to a profit ASAP. Maybe you borrow gear, call in some favors, or barter for space and advertising. Get that cousin who broke your gaming system to work for a week as payback.

• **Crowdfund it**—Tons of people (big and small) have solicited money from "the crowd" to start a business, and there are several popular websites for launching crowdfunding campaigns. Usually, donors get something cool in exchange for their donation. You can raise money quickly, but it takes a lot of pre-planning and a good list of likely donors. More than $6.5 billion has been raised through crowdfunding sites. However, the success rate for fully funding your project is only about 40%. Not bad, but have a backup plan.

• **Borrow it**—Debt can be a powerful tool if used cautiously, and a disaster if used improperly. We've already mentioned credit cards. Certain banks and credit unions offer favorable rates for business start-up loans.

*(Continued on page 77)*

**MAKE FLYERS.** Then print tons of copies and hang them on public bulletin boards, hand them out at school, church, parades, and summer events. Think street marketing (with a trusted adult).

**WEAR YOUR BRAND.** Have a couple of T-shirts made up with your company logo on them. It will be a great conversation starter! Pay your friends in product to do the same.

# STEP 3: CAN YOUR IDEA MAKE MONEY?

**Y**OU'VE got a business idea, now it's time to follow the First Law of Business Success: Make a **profit**. To make a profit, your income must be higher than your expenses (basically it's what's left over after all the bills are paid).

Before you start a biz it's best to figure out if your idea can make a profit. Use a time frame, say a month or a year, over which to estimate your income as a starting point. If you're providing a service, your income is what you charge per hour multiplied by the number of hours you expect to work. If you're providing a product, it's how many items you expect to sell multiplied by the price. Your expenses are the costs of running your business. Calculate everything you'll spend on your business in that month or year. Include the obvious stuff like the cost of supplies, as well as less obvious stuff like the cost of marketing materials. For big purchases, you can spread the cost out over a longer time period. Just divide the total cost by the number of months you plan to pay off the expense, and include one month's worth of the expense in your estimate.

Let's say you buy a $300 lawn mower for your yard-care business and you're going to spread that over the first year of your business. You would divide $300 by 12 months, which equals $25 per month. So you include the $25 as a monthly expense, for 12 months. Then subtract total expenses from total income and you'll have an estimate of whether or not your business can make a profit.

If you get a negative number and it doesn't look like you can make a profit, try adjusting things. Can you get materials cheaper? Can you charge a higher price? Can you reduce your marketing budget? Keep moving stuff around until you come out with a positive number. If it's still not working, try another idea or get some advice. That's the great thing about having a business plan before actually starting a business.

# KID ENTREPRENEURS DOING GOOD

These kids not only started a business, they did some good along the way to help their community. You might say "they done good by doin' good." We wouldn't, because it's horrible grammar, but you get the picture.

## Brown Girls Stationery

At seven years old, Kamaria created a company to make products celebrating young girls of color. Now a teen, Kamaria is the CEO of Brown Girls Stationery and sells backpacks, school supplies, writing paper, notepads, cards, folders, and party supplies. Kamaria finds motivation by building a brand that Black and brown girls can identify with. Next, Kamaria is launching #snackworthy, a nonprofit food distribution business to remind people that just one act of kindness can forever change someone's life for the better.

## Me & the Bees Lemonade

Mikaila was stung by a bee twice in less than a week when she was four years old. Ouch! The experience led Mikaila to learn that bees are pretty amazing and crucial to life on the planet. She also learned that bees are dying off in large numbers.

Mikaila wanted to do something to help the bees and decided to update her great-grandmother's old fashioned lemonade recipe by adding honey instead of sugar. She started selling Me & the Bees Lemonade at her lemonade stand in the front yard, donating a percentage of her profits to organizations working to save the honeybees.

More than 10 years later, business is buzzing. Mikaila has become a book author and motivational speaker, and she teaches workshops on how we can all help save these cute, critical pollinators.

## ManCan

Hart's mom had had enough of her 13-year-old son teasing his sister about her flower-scented candles. So she challenged her son to make "manly" scented candles. Hart accepted the challenge, and ManCan was born—candles poured into used soup cans, with aromas traditionally associated with manliness such as Santa's Beard, Sawdust, Fresh Cut Grass, Burnt Rubber, and, of course, Bacon.

And just like a match to a candle, ManCan caught fire with local and national media, and orders poured in. Today ManCan and SheCan are made by a developmentally disabled workforce in Lisbon, Ohio. ManCan also donates money from the sale of every candle to soup kitchens in Ohio, Pennsylvania, West Virginia, and Michigan.

What started as a joke has turned into a serious business. Hart's efforts not only made him money for college but also won him the Young Entreprenuer of the Year award. Proof once again that you're never too young to make a difference.

# GET A SEPARATE ACCOUNT

**I**F you mix business money together with your personal money, it makes profitability much harder to track. By now you've already opened a personal savings account, so it should be pretty easy to set up a separate business account at the same bank or credit union. Just ask the teller. Also, track every business expense—keep receipts or use an expense tracking app. This will help you whether you're tracking profit or filing your taxes—welcome to the real world of business!

# STEP 4: OPEN YOUR BUSINESS

**H**AVE you nailed the details in your business plan? Good. Now it's time to stop planning and start doing. Make a batch of your product and test it on a friendly audience. Start offering services to all the neighbors you know. Get cracking!

*(Continued from page 74)*

You'd better have a good business plan to help prove the business can make a profit. Also know, no matter whether your business is successful, you'll need to pay that money back, with interest. There are also startup loans that can be secured from the Small Business Association. Google "startup loans" and see what you find. Will a friend or relative loan funds for your business? They'll also want to peek at your business plan, and, like anybody, expect to get paid back. Get the terms of the loan in writing to avoid a potentially awkward Thanksgiving dinner. We strongly suggest the help and advice of a trusted adult in these situations.

• Maybe you use your own $500 for supplies, borrow $500 from Papa for marketing, and crowdfund $500 for equipment. Ya got the funding! Wait, a song is coming to mind . . . "This is how we do it!"

# WHAT IF THINGS GO GREAT?

**Y**OU start your business, and everything goes according to plan. Nice work! Enjoy your success and start saving money to meet your long-term goal of making $1,000,000, but don't rest quite yet.

- **ALWAYS BE ON THE LOOKOUT.** Are there ways to make your product or service better?

- **STAY AHEAD.** To keep up with the competition, do lots of research and talk to your customers to learn about the latest trends.

- **GET HELP.** Pick brains (not literally, of course). Ask friends and family members to pitch in, or even pay someone to help you if you're bringing in enough cash.

- **REINVEST.** Put some of your profits toward marketing, better equipment, and training. It's one of the best ways to make your business (and money) grow.

# WHAT IF THINGS GO NOT-SO-GREAT?

**Y**OU start your business, and not quite everything goes according to plan. You're not making as much money as you hoped. Don't give up!

- **DON'T PANIC.** Keep marketing yourself—success may be closer than you think.

- **ADJUST.** Figure out what's wrong and try to fix it. Are your prices too high? Are you targeting the wrong customers?

- **ENJOY THE RIDE.** Hopefully, your business is based on something you like. Relax, have fun, and see if things pick up.

- **TRY AGAIN.** If your first business idea doesn't work, go back and try something else. The more swings you take, the more hits you'll have.

# DON'T BE AFRAID TO FAIL

**F**IRST business not working out? You're in good company. The difference between success and failure is often a willingness to stick to it. Embrace failing as a stepping stone toward future success. When you make a mistake it's a gift of now knowing what *not* to do in your business. Shrug it off as a learning experience and plan to do better.

## LONG STORY SHORT

*1. Have a business plan and sort out your challenges before you start. Your plan should include the big idea, marketing, how to make a profit, and when to launch.*

*2. Start small and bootstrap your way to making a profit. Try not to blow too much money starting up—that way you get to generate profit a lot faster!*

*3. Keep business separate from personal. Open a separate bank account just for business and keep track of your income and expenses.*

*4. Get out there and promote your products and services!*

# Chapter 8:
# SAVE, SAVE, SAVE

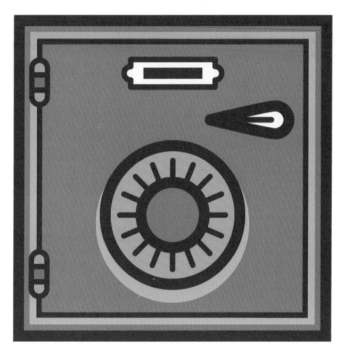

**E**VERYBODY knows how to spend money. You hand over the cash and you get what you want. The problem is having money to hand over in the first place. If all you know how to do is spend money, you'll never become a millionaire.

However, if you save like a millionaire saves, you won't have to save like mad your whole life. You'll have to save up only a fraction of $1,000,000 and let your money do the rest. And the faster you start learning to save, the sooner you'll get to your goal.

# SAVING IS COOL

**S**OME people think saving money is uncool. They think if they *look* like a millionaire, they *are* one. But, sadly, they aren't and may never be. As you grow older, you'll hear story after story of someone who had a lot of money but didn't have the discipline to save it, or even worse: someone who went into thousands of dollars of debt.

Building up a chunk of change can be the *ultimate* cool. And the more you save, the more financial power and self-esteem you build. Train yourself to save. Think of saving money as a life-long game. With a little practice, you can become quite good at it.

# HOW TO SAVE MONEY

## (THE SHORT VERSION)

**D**ON'T spend it. *The End*. Seriously, don't spend it. Thank you.

# HOW TO SAVE MONEY

## (THE LONG VERSION)

**M**AYBE saving money is a *little* bit more complicated than that. In theory, saving is easy: keep the money that is coming in (income) higher than the money going out (expenses). But how do you know when to save and when to spend? How do you keep all those sneaky temptations under control? And how do you protect your big, fat, ever-growing pile of money? The trick is knowing needs from wants.

# GIMME WHAT I NEED, WHAT I REALLY, REALLY NEED

**E**VERY once in a while you'll hear about the student who lived on ramen noodles so he could save up enough money to start his own business. Most people are not born with that kind of self-control. That's where knowing wants from needs comes in.

Needs can be pretty basic: food, water, clothing, and shelter. Wants are things we desire—things we think will make us feel good or make life more convenient or make people notice us. We won't die without them—but we feel a strong desire to spend our money on them. You need water. You want designer fizzy water. You need shelter. You want a mansion. You need transportation. You want a sports car. If you can separate wants from needs, you will have a far easier time making decisions to help you save money. Ask yourself:

*"If I don't get _____, will I actually, physically die?"*

If the answer to the question is no, congratulations! You don't need that thing and you don't have to spend that money. Maybe we're being a little over the top, yet almost everybody wants more than they need. If you can stop yourself from spending when you don't need to, you'll be ahead of the pack.

# BANK ON IT

**W**HEN we talk about saving money, we don't mean hiding some cash in the sock drawer. Why? Saving is hard if there's a big wad of cash burning a hole in your pocket, screaming, "Spend me! Spend me!" in its wee little money voice. Avoid the temptation to spend and shut that money up in a bank or credit union. Why? Because

once you spend your cash it's gone forever. Or you can lose it. Or a family member can "borrow" it and forget to return it! Or it can literally be stolen.

To safely and effectively save money, you have to open a savings account at a bank or credit union. Once set up, start making regular deposits to that account. You can manage it all on your phone and see your balance anytime you want. No more little brother or "best friend" sneaking in and messing with your stash. This is the best way to start saving toward that $1,000,000. We repeat:

## THIS IS THE BEST WAY TO START SAVING TOWARD THAT $1,000,000.

# SAVE IT FOR LATER

There are three important reasons to put your money in a savings account at a bank or credit union:

1. **SAFETY.** Banks and credit unions keep your money safe. Safer than safe. Safer-than-your-piggy-bank kind of safe. It's protected by a government insurance plan. So even if the bank is robbed, your money will be safe and sound.

2. **INTEREST.** Banks will pay you for letting them use your money. Seriously. It's called "interest." We talked about this a little earlier. Both banks and credit unions loan the money you deposit (after holding on to a reserve) to other people or companies for a higher rate of interest. These days, they don't pay very much interest, but it's more than what your money is earning in your sock drawer.

3. **LESS TEMPTATION TO SPEND IT.** There's an old saying: "Out of sight, out of mind." If your money is locked away, you have less temptation to spend it. Having it in a financial institution adds a safeguard against sudden spur-of-the-moment decisions to blow some cash.

# BANK OR CREDIT UNION?

**B**ANKS and credit unions offer many of the same products or services, but there are some differences.

**Banks** are for-profit and earn money for shareholders (people who own stock in the bank). Banks offer a wide range of services from savings and checking accounts to a variety of investment options. Virtually all savings accounts at most banks are insured by the FDIC, or Federal Deposit Insurance Corporation, in case your money is lost or stolen.

**Credit unions** are not-for-profit and are owned by members (the customers of the credit union). Their main mission is to serve their members. That means they may sometimes pay more interest on savings accounts and charge lower fees than many banks. Anyone can become a member of a credit union, but some are available only to people living in the state where they are located. All credit unions have checking and savings accounts and some have a larger list of services, like small business and home loans. Your money is also insured, much like a bank, through the NCUA, or National Credit Union Administration.

If you want a fee-free ATM on every corner, a big national bank might be best for you. If you want higher interest and lower fees, consider a credit union. The important thing is to make the right choice for your financial goals.

**SKIP THE SOCK DRAWER.**

belongs to you. It will when you turn 18 (or 21, again, depending on the state where you live).

Here are some other important things to know about custodial accounts:

- The money in a custodial account belongs to you by law. However, the custodian is the only one who can perform transactions.

- Many custodial accounts make it easy for the account owner (that's you!) to check your balance on your phone.

# OPEN A SAVINGS ACCOUNT

**O**NE type of savings account is called a **custodial account**. If you're under 18 (or 21, depending on where you live) you'll need a parent or guardian to help you open this type of account. That grown-up is called the custodian, and just as the custodian at your school maintains the building, the custodian of your savings account maintains your money (only with less mopping). Make sure the custodian you pick is someone you really trust! Hopefully, that person will let you make as many decisions as possible about your money, so it's really like the savings account

350

*If you stack up a million one-dollar bills, it would be 350 feet tall (that's 107 meters for readers in most of the world). Start stacking your money in a savings account today!*

# IN-SCHOOL CREDIT UNIONS

Did you know there are more than 900 in-school credit unions around the country? That's a credit union right inside your school for students, run by students. Talk about easy access to lunch money! Most offer just savings and checking accounts, but if you're lucky enough to be a member of one of these, then you might not need a custodian on the account. If you'd like a credit union set up in your high school, contact us at bizkids.com.

• A custodial savings account is designed for saving money. You can withdraw only a certain number of times per month or you get dinged with a fee.

The important thing is to open an account now! It might be the credit union around the corner (because you don't drive), or the bank with the most ATMs, or you can take the easy route and just use the same financial institution as your parents. Can you say "Direct deposit my allowance, please!"?

# PAY YOURSELF FIRST

WE know we talked about this earlier, but it is so important we need to bring it up again. Hmm, what to do with your allowance? There's that new game to download, those new jeans, and you really "need" a new phone. How can you ever save anything if you're always paying for stuff?

The answer is, you don't—you pay yourself first (or PYF, for short), every time.

PYF means every time money lands in your pocket, you put some of it away in your savings account before

*Pay yourself first: It's the easiest trick in the book. Don't forget it! Write it down! Type it up! Write it in needlework!*

PAY
YOURSELF
FIRST

you spend any of it. Basically, you make your savings goal *numero uno* before you start spending. It can be a certain dollar amount, like $10 per paycheck, or a percentage, say, 20% of your allowance. It should be included in your budget and be paid *first*. That's part of the PYF strategy: You make sure the money intended for your savings account hits the bank before you hit the stores!

And what's the easiest way to do the easiest trick in this book? Make it automatic. That means set up an automatic transfer every month from one account into a separate savings account. You can set this up through your bank or credit union. Maybe every month you transfer your monthly savings goal into a separate account, as an easy way to reach your goal (then you won't be tempted to spend it). Just remember to have enough money in your first account to do the transfer!

## SAVING NOW = POWER LATER

**B**E consistent. It is crucial that you make regular deposits to your savings account, no matter how small, weekly or monthly. Keep it up. You might go three months or even six before you start noticing that you've "got money in the bank." But pretty soon, saving will become a habit. You just won't feel right until you've put a little bit of money away each week. Even with small amounts, if you make saving a habit, over time that balance will grow, and grow, and grow! To get you started, here are some savings tricks of the rich and famous (and not-so-famous):

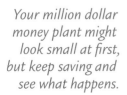

*Your million dollar money plant might look small at first, but keep saving and see what happens.*

# QUESTIONS TO ASK WHEN CHOOSING A BANK OR CREDIT UNION

When choosing a financial institution compare interest rates, fees, services, and incentives. Then pick the bank or credit union that's best for you. There could be some conditions in the fine print, so remember to ask these questions:

• What interest rates do you pay on savings accounts? (It's going to be low, but that's OK for now.)

• What monthly fees do you charge on savings or checking accounts?

• How much do you charge if I over-draw my account? ("Insufficient Funds" fees can be charged to you if you spend more than what's in your account. These can really hurt. Like hundreds of dollars' worth of hurt. So, think like a millionaire and always keep a minimum balance in your account.)

• What's the minimum amount I need to open an account?

• How many branch locations do you have?

• Where are your ATMs located?

• What features are offered on your banking app and online banking interface?

• Are you insured by the FDIC (banks) or the NCUA (credit unions) . . . just in case someone robs the bank!

- Save unexpected windfalls. Put that twenty bucks your uncle sent you right in the bank.

- Avoid impulse buys.

- Track your spending in a budget.

- Always be thinking of ways to cut your expenses.

- Use round-up apps that automatically put the difference between a purchase and the next dollar into a savings account. You won't even miss it!

- Leave debit cards and credit cards (if you're old enough to have them) at home—use cash instead. You'll spend less.

- Never pay full price—use the Internet to research the best deals.

- Bring lunch to school instead of spending money.

- Shop around for financial institutions with the best interest rates. The difference in rates won't seem like much, but 1% is still double 0.5%, so you might as well try to get the best you can because it all adds up.

# THE BEST THINGS IN LIFE ARE FREE!

Becoming a millionaire means *not* spending your money. Does that mean *not* having fun? Far from it. Just go online and search for free activities where you live. You'll find tons of ways to kill some time without killing your wallet. Here are some ideas:

- Most museums have a free day during the month.

- Nature is almost always free. Get something to throw or kick and head for the park.

- See what's new at the library. Check out the latest issues of all the financial publications, magazines, and movies. And these things called books! All free!

- Create a "Cheap Club" with friends. The club meets once a month and the hosts are tasked with coming up with food and entertainment on a very stingy budget, like $5 per person.

# FLEX THOSE SAVINGS MUSCLES

Just like a bodybuilder makes a habit of lifting weights, to reach your savings goal, you'll need to make a habit of saving money. So get creative, get disciplined, and pump some muscle into your savings account. If you make a few mistakes along the way, no worries. A few sacrifices here and there will get you back on track.

($212.62 closer to your $500 goal and eventually, $1,000,000!)

More interest earned!

**SHORT TERM GOAL =** Save **$500** in **one year**

Open savings account and make first deposit. Yay!

Leave debit card at home and use cash only.

Go to mall with friends and blow budget.

($1.73 Hey, every little bit helps!)

Earn interest.

**Pay Yourself First.** Make deposits into savings account every Friday.

(-$37.52)

**FREE DAY!** Play frisbee with friends instead of going to the mall.

Start spending diary.

($11 added)

Deposit extra money into account.

(No matter how small!)

Buy used books for school.

(save $78)

Get MDM back! Sell old clothes online to make up for budget blunder.

(save $21)

Postpone going to movies next month.

Bring lunch to school.

**BACK ON TRACK!**

($27 back in my pocket)

Money is tight this month. Take extra babysitting job.

(save $6.41)

Research best online deals for makeup.

(save $5)

Deposit entire allowance this month!

(save $5)

Bring lunch to school.

($45)

(Woo-hoo! $50 added)

# START TODAY!

**O**K, maybe we're beginning to sound like a broken **record** (for those of you who don't know what a record is, check the glossary), but none of the information in this book will matter if you don't think like a millionaire and start saving today.

Can you condition your mind and discipline yourself to control your spending? Can you pay yourself first on a regular basis? Can you be patient and keep saving? Yes? Good, because, at first, the amounts you're saving may seem teeny and insignificant. Then one day you'll wake up and notice you have a thousand bucks in your savings account. Stand by because we're about to share the not-so-secret secret to launch you on your way to being a real millionaire!

# LONG STORY SHORT

1. *Think about not spending money.*

2. *Know the difference between wants and needs.*

3. *Open a savings account and make regular deposits, and save, save, save!*

4. *Pay yourself first (PYF).*

5. *Did we mention save, save, save?*

# Chapter 9:
# THE POWER OF COMPOUND INTEREST

**E**INSTEIN never said "compound interest is the most powerful force in the universe." But if he had, he'd be right. **Compound interest** is the most powerful force in the universe. OK, the point can be argued, but in the case of this book, compound interest is, dare we say it, *The Most Powerful Force in the Universe* if you are going to grow your money from $100 to $1,000,000.

Got your attention? Thought so.

# QUESTION:

Which would you rather have?

**A.** $1,000,000

**B.** One penny, doubled every day, for a month. (One penny the first day, then two pennies the next, then four pennies the third day, then eight pennies on the fourth day, and so on, and so on. . . .)

C'mon, you know this is a setup. Do the math!

**HINT:** The answer has something to do with the power of compounding.

OK
Answer A isn't bad, but you want to pick Answer B. One penny, doubled every day for a month, is $5,368,709.12! Holy Compound Interest, Mr. Lincoln!

# STAND BY FOR THE SECRET

**W**HEN you put your money in a savings account, in a way you're lending money to the bank. Remember when we told you the bank pays you a little something called interest to encourage you to keep your money there (instead of buying a hundred pounds of Red Vines)? Good.

Imagine that you have $100 in a savings account earning **simple interest**. That interest is based on the **principal** (the money you have in the account), in this case $100. Let's say your $100 is earning 5% interest per year, and you're not adding any more money to the

account. That means you would earn $5 the first year, $5 the second year, and so on. After 10 years you'll have $150 in your account.

# HERE COMES MIND BLOWING!

**W**ITH compound interest you earn *interest on your interest*. Yes, it's true! Now imagine that you have $100 principal in an account earning compound interest at the same 5% per year. You would still earn $5 the first year, for a total of $105, but by the second year, things would start to get interesting. The compound interest paid is based on the principal ($100)

# COMPOUND INTEREST FORMULA

Here is the official mathematical formula for compound interest. Go ahead, Einstein, figure it out:

$$A = P \left(1 + \frac{R}{N}\right)^{NT}$$

where:

**A** = amount accumulated

**P** = principal amount (initial investment)

**R** = annual nominal interest rate (not reflecting the compounding)

**N** = number of times the interest is compounded per year

**NT** = number of years the money is borrowed for

# THE RULE OF 72

Want a quick way to determine how many years it will take to double your money? Use the **rule of 72**! Just divide 72 by the fixed annual interest rate. It's not perfectly accurate, but it will put you in the ballpark for interest rates less than 20%. For example, if you invest $100 at 10% per year, you would divide 72 by 10: 72/10 = 7.2 years.

So it will take approximately 7.2 years to double your money, if you can earn an average of 10% interest per year—challenging but not impossible.

# MONEY MOMENT

Compound interest can also be used against you. When it comes to credit cards and compound interest, time is not on your side. Credit card companies are using compound interest to calculate what you owe. And it's high—usually somewhere from 12% to 30%! The longer you have the debt, the more the interest grows.

plus the $5 interest from that first year. So you're actually being paid 5% on $105. That would be $110.25. In the third year, compound interest would be paid on the original $100 plus two years' worth of interest, or $115.51. In 10 years, instead of having just $150 to show for your saving efforts, you'd have $162.89. That is almost 9% more money over the same time period because you earned interest on your interest.

# WHAT THIS MEANS TO YOU

This means that if you want to eventually have $1,000,000, you don't actually have to save up one million $1 bills. You need to save up only enough money so that, over time, your money begins to work for you, earning compound interest.

# WHAT'S THE CATCH?

COMPOUND interest isn't magic—it's just math. As your amount of principal and interest builds up, your total amount of money starts to grow faster and faster and faster.

*(Continued on page 101)*

# TIME REALLY IS MONEY

The earlier you let that compound interest train get rollin', the faster and bigger you can build your money. Going back to the example of $100 in savings, let's imagine you left that money in a savings account at 5% and just ignored it. With simple interest, in 50 years, you'd have $350. That's pretty good, considering you didn't have to lift a finger. But with compound interest, you'd have a whopping $1,146.74! All from your original hundred bucks! Look what happens when your original investment of $100 is actually $1,000 and we change the interest rate to 10%.

## COMPOUND INTEREST 10% for 50 YEARS

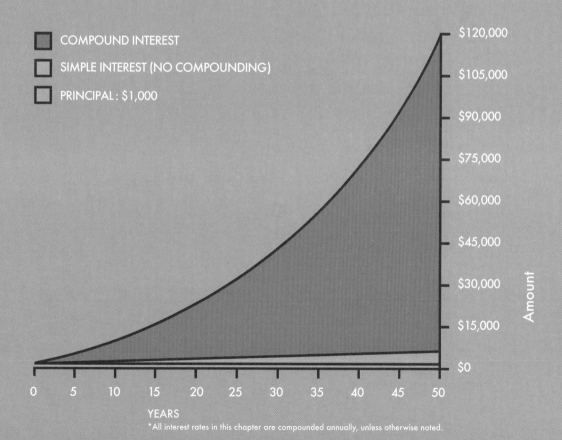

☐ COMPOUND INTEREST
☐ SIMPLE INTEREST (NO COMPOUNDING)
☐ PRINCIPAL : $1,000

*All interest rates in this chapter are compounded annually, unless otherwise noted.

# THE SECRET WITHIN THE SECRET

While compound interest on the principal alone is pretty powerful, see what happens when you keep adding money to the principal on a regular basis. Things skyrocket! Take a look at both these examples:

Jamie and Erren, both 15 years old, each start with an initial investment of $5,000 saved up from their jobs, allowances, a birthday gift from Uncle Joe, and odd jobs for neighbors. Both save for 50 years and are able to earn an average of 8% return on their money. Jamie doesn't make any more contributions after her initial $5,000, but Erren continues to make yearly contributions of $1,000 to her account (that's $83.33 per month, which is doable for most adults).

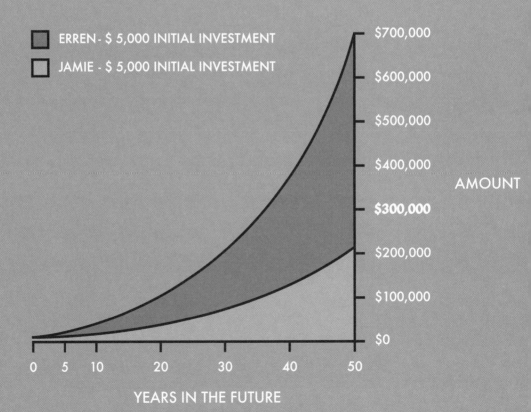

How to Turn $100 into $1,000,000

Wow! Look at the difference adding money to the principal made over the long term. Erren was able to grow her money exponentially, just by saving an extra $83.33 per month for 50 years. In just a few more years, she will reach $1,000,000. Impressive, huh?

Jackson and Layla want to become millionaires. Jackson started saving $1,000 per year at 15 years old. He was able to earn an average of 8% interest on his investments. Layla didn't start saving until she was 30 years old. Because Jackson was able to take advantage of the power of compound interest over a longer period of time, he was able to get to $1,000,000 with less money— $85,000 *less* to be exact. Where Jackson invested $55,000 over the long term, Layla had to invest $140,000 to reach the same amount because she waited. Start saving as much as you can, as young as you can, to take full advantage of the power of compound interest.

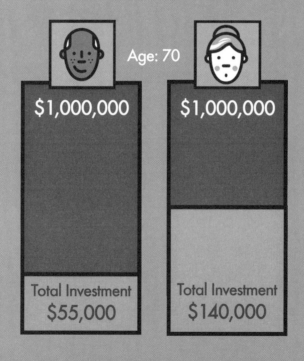

Age: 70

$1,000,000

$1,000,000

Total Investment
$55,000

Total Investment
$140,000

Jackson started saving when he was 15.

Layla didn't start saving until she was 30.

Both reach $1,000,000 by age 70 but Layla's total investment was $140,000. And Jackson only had to invest $55,000.

While savings accounts are a great place to stash your cash, you will eventually have to move money into other accounts and investments that will compound at a higher interest rate. This will become your portfolio, which is just a fancy way of saying your "collection" of investments. We explain them more in the next chapter, but here's an example of compound interest at work when various investments are in the picture:

Georgia saves up $55,000 by the time she's 40. Look at the huge difference earning a higher percent of interest makes on her investment over the next 35 years.

If she left her $55,000 in a **CD** that earned 3% interest, after 35 years it would be $154,762.43. If instead she invested her $55,000 in bonds that returned on average 6% interest, then she would have $422,734.77. Wow! But take a look at what would happen if she invested her money in the stock market and was able to get a 9% return on her money—her investment almost triples to $1,122,768.24. Turns out Georgia is a really smart investor and was able to get an average of 12% return on her stock picks, and her mere $55,000 turns into a whopping $2,903,979.08, all due to the power of compound interest.

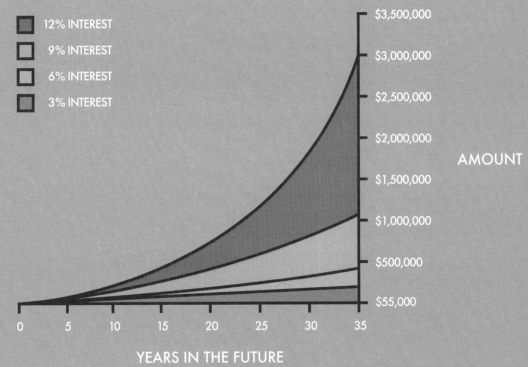

*(Continued from page 96)*

But don't stop adding money to the account—or worse, take any money out—or you'll lose the power of compounding. Keep adding money to the account or investment on a regular basis. Over time, your money will grow bigger, faster. Bottom line: When it comes to saving up a million dollars, you want to keep the pedal to the metal. Take a look at how much you'd have to save each month (approximately) to get $1,000,000, depending on how soon you want to reach your goal—30, 40, or 50 years (assumes annual interest at 8% compounded annually*).

 *Reach $1,000,000 in 30 years =*
*must save $706 a month*
*TOTAL INVESTMENT = $254,160*

 *Reach $1,000,000 in 40 years =*
*must save $309 a month*
*TOTAL INVESTMENT = $148,320*

 *Reach $1,000,000 in 50 years =*
*must save $140 a month*
*TOTAL INVESTMENT = $84,000.*

*\* Taxes and inflation have not been factored into results.*

# NOW YOU KNOW THE SECRET

**C**OMPOUND interest is the secret to saving up $1,000,000. It may involve a little math, but you don't need to be good with numbers to make $1,000,000, just good at saving money.

And it doesn't take an Einstein (like that segue?) to understand why it's important to start saving as young as you can. If compound interest is not the most powerful force in the entire universe, it is at least in the financial universe.

# LONG STORY SHORT

· · · · · · · · · · · · · · · · · · · · · · · · · · · · · ·

*With compound interest, your money makes money and the money your money makes makes more money.*

# Chapter 10:
# INVESTING

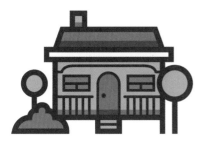

**B**Y now you have hopefully achieved your short-term goal of saving up $100. Maybe you've been so inspired from reading this book that you've already saved up $10,000! Congratulations!

A savings account is a great place to stash your money at first. But it won't make you $1,000,000—not in your lifetime anyway.

Getting to $1,000,000 requires moving some of your money from a basic savings account into investments that offer a higher **rate of return**. How much more? Many financial advisers suggest

# WHO IS WARREN BUFFETT?

With a net worth in the billions of dollars, Warren Buffett is one of the wealthiest people in the world, and one of the most successful investors in history. Buffett is big on "Dollar Cost Averaging": investing the same amount of money into well-researched investments every month over a long period of time, no matter what the market is doing. DCA is a great way to ride out market downturns and to avoid the risks of emotional investing. Go online and search "investing tips for beginners" by Warren Buffett and you'll find a treasure trove of advice, such as "Dividends are your friend. Buy and hold. Be fearful when others are greedy and greedy when others are fearful." Despite his wealth, Buffett drives an old Cadillac and still lives in the same house he bought 50 years ago. Talk about frugality! More impressive, though, is his pledge to give away 99% of his money.

your Benjamins should be growing, on average, somewhere between 5% and 12% per year. NEWSFLASH: You'll never get that from a savings account.

Of course, it's not quite that simple. You have to work for high-interest investment returns. More important, investments aren't insured like your savings account. You risk losing everything if your investment decreases in value. Smart investors only invest money they're willing to lose.

# WHAT IS INVESTING?

INVESTING means putting your money into something that can potentially make you *more* money. And the number of places where you can invest your money is staggering.

You can invest in just about anything. Anything! Enjoy skateboarding? You can invest in a company that makes skateboards or skateboard shoes. You can also invest in the company that makes the concrete in the

*You can inve in just about anything, and we mea anything—j make sure i increases in value over ti*

skate park. You can even invest in the company that makes the fuel for the ambulance that carries your friend to the hospital after that missed plasma spin.

Whatever you invest in, you want it to be something that will become more valuable over time so your investment grows. Hopefully, as skateboarding becomes more popular, more skateboards are sold, and your investment in the skateboard company eventually becomes more valuable.

# RISK AND REWARD

LIKE skateboarding, investing means taking a risk in the hope of a reward. In skateboarding, when you learn a new trick, you risk smacking the pavement for the reward of becoming a better skater. When you invest your money, you take the risk of kissing your money good-bye for the reward of possibly making more money. Are you willing to take that risk?

# WHEN SHOULD YOU START?

NO longer do you have to build up a chunk of change or find a broker to invest in the stock market. Today, there are investing apps galore that have democratized investing, making it accessible for everyone. Anyone with a smartphone and a bank account can invest in the stock market. You can even use apps that round up the difference in your $6.63 donut purchase to the nearest dollar, and boom! You've invested $0.37 in Apple. But you know what hasn't changed? This still stands the test of time: don't risk money you'll eventually need (like college tuition). So before you start investing, ask yourself, "Self, how much money am I comfortable with risking?" (Hint: All of it? No. Some of it? Yes.) No matter how small your initial investment may be, this will become your investment portfolio. Eventually, it will include

*(Continued on page 108)*

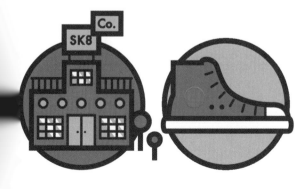

# THINGS PEOPLE INVEST IN

You can invest in almost anything. Here are some common investments that range in risk:

## CDs, OR CERTIFICATES OF DEPOSIT

Certificates of Deposit (CDs) are available at banks and credit unions, and are low risk, but offer very low reward (not much more interest than a savings account). CDs require you to keep the funds invested for a set period of time, like 6 months or a few years.

## STOCKS

You become part owner of a **public company** that offers goods or services when you buy **shares** (aka "stock") in that company. You can invest in anything from "penny" stocks (high risk) to blue chip stocks (lower risk).

## CRYPTOCURRENCY

Cryptocurrency is a new form of digital money that is secured by blockchain technology, which makes it nearly impossible to counterfeit or double-spend. NFTs (non-fungible tokens) are a unique digital representation of an asset like artwork or real estate, and can't be replicated. The trading of crypto and NFTs may be a way to create future wealth, but it's highly risky. So far investors have made millions . . . and lost millions.

## BONDS

You loan money to a company, or the government, with a promise that it will be repaid with interest. Bonds are rated by credit agencies according to how risky they are, from AAA (low risk) to NR (not rated or high risk).

## REAL ESTATE

You can invest directly in residential property (like your parents' home) or commercial property (like a shopping mall). Or you can invest indirectly through real estate investment trusts (REITs), which are traded as a stock on the various stock exchanges.

## COMMODITIES

Commodities are raw materials that are used to make other things: precious metals (gold, silver, copper, etc.), coffee beans, lumber, oil—even pork bellies! Investors don't usually buy and sell commodities themselves but purchase a contract to buy them at a certain price.

## COMPANIES

You can invest in a company directly by lending the owners money or becoming one of the owners yourself. This is risky, but it can also produce high returns.

## ART AND ANTIQUES

The right piece of art can appreciate faster than almost any investment on the planet, but it has to be the right piece. Sometimes even a half-shredded painting can command millions of dollars.

*(Continued from page 105)*

a combination of different types of investments. Choose wisely and see if your investment goes up in value. If so, great! If not, don't panic. Ask why. Did you make the right investment? Maybe it just needs a little more time. You will make some mistakes with your investments, especially at first. Don't be discouraged. Even the most experienced investors lose money. The key is to make more money than you lose. You increase your chances of doing that by taking your time and doing your research.

## STOCK BASICS 101

**Y**OU can invest in a lot of different things, but many people start with stocks. They're easy to buy, sell, and understand. They also historically outperform other investment options over the long-term.

A public company can raise money by selling portions of ownership called shares to the public through a **stock market**. (**Private companies** don't sell stock to the general public.) Buying a share of stock makes you a "shareholder," and you become a partial owner of that company. The company gets money to grow and you get to own a piece of a company. From railroads to space travel, shoelaces to software, the list of public companies that issue stock is huge!

Stocks are bought and sold. One person is buying a stock that they think will go up in value, while another person is selling that stock because they think it will go down (or they need money).

Stock prices represent the battle between those two thoughts. Who's right? Who knows? Multiply this by millions of shares of stock being bought and sold by millions of people every day, and you have a stock market.

## BUY IT!

**Y**OU have a lot of choices these days when it comes to actually buying stock. In the olden days you had to open an account at a brokerage firm and a broker would buy and sell the stock for you. And in exchange for that transaction they would charge a nice little **commission** fee. You can still buy stocks the old-school way, but modern trading apps streamline the process of buying and selling shares. Either way, you still need to keep an eye out on the fees charged—if you're hoping to make 9% interest but are being charged 2.5% fees for every transaction, you're actually only making 6.5% interest. Here are three important things to keep in mind:

**1.** Your money is not insured like it is with a savings account. Choose a well-established company you can trust.

**2.** Trading stocks costs money, so try to choose a brokerage with low fees. The less you pay, the more you keep!

**3.** Choose a brokerage that lets you purchase partial shares (also called fractional shares). That means you can buy as much or as little of a stock as you want—even less than one share. With some stocks trading at hundreds of dollars a share, that can be a good thing!

# CHOOSING YOUR FIRST STOCK

**T**HERE are literally thousands of stocks to choose from. How do you go about picking your first one? If you want to invest in individual stocks, a good way to start is with companies you know. What is your favorite beverage? What shoes are you wearing? What snacks do you eat? Any of those businesses could be **listed** on a stock exchange. All you have to do is find the company's stock exchange symbol, and do some research. (*Never buy a stock without doing your research.*) You might also look at the top ten performing

# BULL VS. BEAR

What is the long-term performance history of the stock market? Throughout stock market history, the average yearly return for periods of 25 years or longer has been between 9% and 10%. When stock prices are rising the market is said to be a **bull market**, and when it's on a downward trend it's said to be a **bear market**. The terms *bear* and *bull* are thought to originate from how each animal attacks its opponents. That is, a bull will thrust its horns up into the air, whereas a bear will swipe down.

# ALPHABET SOUP

If you read the financial news, you might come across what seems like a bowl of alphabet soup: NYSE, NASDAQ, DOW. Here's how to make sense of it all:

Stocks are bought and sold on an **exchange**, and the two largest ones in the world are:

• **THE NEW YORK STOCK EXCHANGE** (known as **NYSE**, but don't ever pronounce it as "nice-ee")

• **THE NATIONAL ASSOCIATION OF SECURITIES DEALERS AUTOMATED QUOTATIONS** (always called the **NASDAQ**, pronounced "nazz-dak")

What about those other letters you often hear? Like S&P 500 and the Dow? They are referring to an **index**. An index is like an imaginary grouping of stocks and can be a good indicator as to whether the market as a whole is going up or down. Two well-known indices are:

• **S&P 500:** "S&P" stands for **STANDARD AND POOR'S**, which is a **rating agency**. It recommends which stocks to buy and sell and also keeps track of the S&P 500. True to its name, it's based on 500 stocks and is the most commonly used benchmark for the health of the stock market.

• **DOW:** When people say "the Dow" they mean the **DOW JONES INDUSTRIAL AVERAGE.** It's similar to the S&P, except it tracks 30 really big companies. To be included in this index, a stock must be a leader in its industry and widely held by investors.

Watch these indices and get a sense for where the stock market is going overall. It pays to keep an eye on the general state of the market.

companies over the past few months or years. Pay particular attention to ones that have weathered **economic downturns**.

Your goal is to find good companies that will go up in value—not the one making the coolest thing. A cool company doesn't equal a great investment. That's where doing your research as a young investor comes into play.

# HOW DO YOU ACTUALLY MAKE MONEY?

**B** **OUGHT** your first stock? Congrats! Time is on your side, so hold on to your stock while it hopefully goes up in value. The key to profiting from an individual stock is to **buy low and sell high**. If the stock costs $10 and it goes up $2 over the course of a year, your investment has risen 20%. That's if you were to sell it. If you hold on to it, it may keep rising and may go up another $2 the next year. When you decide to sell your stock, the number of shares times the price you sell them for (minus the brokerage fees) gets deposited into your account.

Finding **undervalued** stocks and waiting until everyone else catches on is called **value investing**. It is a very

# DO YOUR RESEARCH

There's a lot to research about each stock. The more experienced investor will want to know details like **P/E ratios** and **market capitalization**, but here are some important basics to consider:

- Profitability: Is the company making a profit or will it be able to soon?
- Growth prospects: Is the company expanding into new markets or hiring more employees?
- Management: Do the key executives (aka bosses) have the experience to reach the company's goals?
- Competitive Advantage: Does the company have a special or unique advantage compared to its competitors?

Finally, always remember that past performance is not a guarantee of future results.

PRO TIP: There are tons of stock investing games with imaginary money. Try them out and avoid a bunch of rookie mistakes before risking your real cash.

popular investing style. It involves researching companies to understand their strengths and any risks they have, and then deciding if the stock price is fair. In many cases, strong but boring companies do not get as much attention from investors. A value investor would see this, buy the stock, and wait for its value to go up.

# STOCK SPLITS

**O**CCASIONALLY, a company will authorize a splitting of the stock. It will do this to keep the price attractive to new investors and to reward current ones. It can vary, but many stocks will split 2 for 1. That means for every share you own, you now own two at half the original share price. Hopefully, the stock will rise back to the original price, and you can potentially double your money.

# DELIGHTFUL DIVIDENDS

**S**OME companies pay a **dividend** on their stock. Dividends are a share of the company's profits that the company gives back to investors.

Dividend payments are usually made once every three months. They can often be fairly substantial—several percentage points of a stock's price (much more than you'd earn with a savings account). Dividends are paid per share, so the more shares you own, the more you collect. One more thing: Some financial analysts think dividend-paying stocks tend to do better over the long term. So a company with stocks that pay dividends may be worth an extra look.

# DON'T BE SHY— DIVERSIFY!

**E**VER heard the saying "Don't put all your eggs in one basket"? You don't want to own just one investment. You want to diversify. **Diversification** just means owning a bunch of different stocks in different industries, and often mixing in other investment types as well. Why is diversification important? Because it spreads out your risk. The price of a single stock can change a lot from day to day. But when you add a whole bunch of stocks together, those swings are usually not as wild—and if they are, the entire market is doing it, too.

# FUN WITH FUNDS

**A** great way to diversify is to invest in multiple stocks at once using **mutual funds** and **index funds.**

• A mutual fund is an investment that packages together many types of investments. Some might hold only stocks; others might add bonds, real estate, or precious metals and other commodities to the mix.

• An index fund follows the total performance of a group of stocks. For example, SPY is the symbol for an index fund that follows the S&P 500.

# SILLY SYMBOLS

Every company on a stock exchange is represented by a symbol. It's usually a few letters representing the company's full name, but some companies get clever.

**STEINWAY (LVB):** Piano maker honors famous pianist Ludwig van Beethoven

**OLYMPIC STEEL (ZEUS):** Steel manufacturer pays homage to a Greek god

**MARKET VECTORS AGRIBUSINESS ETF (MOO):** Must be in the cow business

**HARLEY DAVIDSON (HOG):** Motorcycle company plays up its famous nickname

**ASIA TIGER FUND (GRR):** Investment fund that sounds like an angry tiger

**DYNAMIC MATERIALS (BOOM):** Hmm . . . wonder if dynamite is involved?

**NATIONAL BEVERAGE (FIZZ):** Playful and catchy symbol for a beverage company

*When you're young, you have time for your money to grow, and can take more risks and make mistakes, but when you get older you'll need to protect yourself.*

Both kinds of funds can have a very broad range of stocks, or a very narrow one. There are funds that focus on technology, on socially responsible companies, or even ones that are just made up of stocks that pay dividends.

Some funds are run by people who do a lot of the research for you. You often pay a hefty fee for their expertise in the form of a "management fee." One thing to remember is that a fund can function like a rollercoaster—what has been great for the past five years could tank the next. Sometimes smart fund managers just turn out to be lucky ones—and good luck can turn into bad.

Other funds—especially index funds—are controlled by committees and/or algorithms, which are rules that automatically determine which stocks or bonds will be in the fund. Because there's no human brainiac managing them, index funds often charge lower management fees. These funds can be good options for people who aren't willing to pay big fees up front

Before you invest in a fund, carefully read the details of the investment offering (called a **prospectus**). Make sure to read the fine print: Some funds charge little or nothing, making them a great deal for the beginning investor (assuming they go up!). Others charge hefty fees that can take a serious bite out of your profits.

The great thing about mutual funds and index funds is that they let you "own" a whole bunch of different stocks with every share you buy. That means you achieve instant diversification.

# KNOW WHEN TO HOLD 'EM, KNOW WHEN TO FOLD 'EM

**T**IME is on your side. If you buy a stock and it goes down, you don't have to sell it right away. The same is true if the stock goes up. If you did your research and it's a solid company, you could try holding on to it and seeing where it goes. Stocks go up and down all the time—you don't earn or lose money until you sell the stock or the company goes out of business (yes, it happens). If it is a good quality stock, investors who hold over the long term are more likely to win out in the end.

How to Turn $100 into $1,000,000

# CAPITAL GAINS

**C**APITAL **gains taxes** are taxes paid on profits from selling stocks. If you buy and then sell a stock less than a year later, the gains are taxed higher than if you hold the stock for more than a year. Before you sell your stock, find out the tax implications. You might talk to a broker or an accountant about this because taxes can vary by state. For kids who don't earn much income during the year, it may not make much of an impact.

# WHERE TO RESEARCH

- **STOCK WEBSITES:** Big stock market websites have news, analyst reports, and historical charts for just about every stock across all the big exchanges. Some examples include: Investopedia, Motley Fool, Yahoo! Finance, The Street, and MSN Money.

- **FINANCIAL APPS:** Even if you don't understand all the investing lingo, investing apps are a great way to learn and figure out what you might want to invest in. With easy-to-use interfaces and low fees, these apps cater to the everyday investor who may not be a financial wizard.

- **COMPANY QUARTERLY EARNING REPORTS:** All publicly listed companies file a report on their earnings and **losses** at the end of each quarter. Read them before you invest.

- **FRIENDS AND FAMILY:** Ask people you know if they invest, what they invest in, and why.

# ADVENTURES IN INVESTING

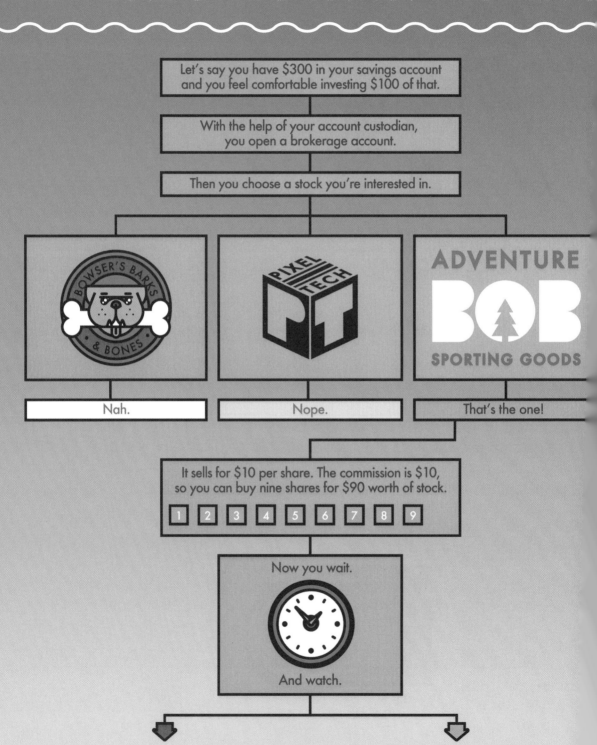

Let's say you have $300 in your savings account and you feel comfortable investing $100 of that.

With the help of your account custodian, you open a brokerage account.

Then you choose a stock you're interested in.

BOWSER'S BARKS & BONES

PIXEL TECH

ADVENTURE BOB SPORTING GOODS

Nah.

Nope.

That's the one!

It sells for $10 per share. The commission is $10, so you can buy nine shares for $90 worth of stock.

| 1 | 2 | 3 | 4 | 5 | 6 | 7 | 8 | 9 |

Now you wait.

And watch.

If the stock goes up, decide whether to keep it and hope it goes up more, or sell it and TAKE A PROFIT.

If the stock goes down, decide whether to hold on to it and hope it changes direction, or give up, sell it and TAKE A LOSS.

Let's assume you made a good pick—the stock goes up 10% after a year! 10% of $90 is $9. Now you have $99 worth of stock.

What are your options?

### SELL
You decide to sell the stock. But you forgot about that pesky commission! $99 minus $10 is $89. You started with $100, and your stock went up, but you still lost $11.

### HOLD
You hold on to the stock for another year. The company does great, and your stock grows another 10%. Now your stock is worth $108.90. Here's the catch: You still can't make a profit because of that $10 commission. You can either keep on holding the stock for a few more years, or you can sell it and try to buy something more profitable (although if you're making 10% per year on any investment, you're doing pretty well!).

Let's say the company has a bad year and the stock loses 20% of its value. Yow! That stinks! Now it's worth only $72. What should you do?

YOUR STOCK
$ELL

### SELL
You decide to sell the stock. With the commission fee, you end up with only $62 to your name. You lost more than 30% of your money, but now you can try to invest it in something more profitable. Best of luck to you!

### HOLD
You hang tight, hoping that the stock will rise to its former value. In fact, you hold on to it for 20 years. It has its ups and downs, but over time it does regain its value and then some.

# GAMESTOP

GameStop Corp. is an American video game and consumer electronics company whose stock was hovering around $20 in early January 2021. Many hedge funds (pooled investment funds at large companies) had bought short positions on the stock assuming it would go down in value. However, a coordinated effort by a community of small, independent investors on Reddit, under the subgroup r/wallstreetbets, managed to pump up the stock 1,500% to a high of $483 within two weeks. When those hedge fund investors saw their stock bet heading in the opposite direction it triggered a "short squeeze," forcing them to back out and causing billions in losses. It was a classic "David and Goliath" story that created a commotion in the stock market and captivated the world.

# INVESTING: TALES FROM THE CRYPTO . . . OH!

CRYPTOCURRENCY is a "decentralized" form of digital money and doesn't take the physical form of coins or paper notes. It also isn't controlled by one country, government, or organization. It's a digital form of money that is available to everyone. By now, who hasn't heard of Bitcoin? Created in 2009, it was the first and most popular cryptocurrency. Now, there are over 1,000 types of crypto! Although the value of crypto has risen and fallen like a state fair roller coaster, many people think cryptocurrency will be the money of the future.

How do you know if crypto transactions are legit? What about double-counting? Or hackers? Well, for one thing, all cryptocurrency transactions are recorded through blockchain technology, using cryptographical functions to verify financial transactions (still with us?). In other words, the transactions are extremely secure and open for everyone to see. If you ever need some light bedtime reading, try reviewing the distributed ledger, which records all the crypto transactions in the universe. You'll be asleep in no time.

Why is crypto better? It's secure, it's transparent, and there are lower fees charged for transactions. Why is crypto not better? Crypto currencies are not legally accepted everywhere. So far, only some businesses accept them. Sure, it can come in handy if you are buying a Tesla, but you can't use it to buy a hamburger at McDonald's (at least, not yet).

People buy and trade cryptocurrencies just like stocks or other investments. It's a very risky investment because crypto isn't insured by the FDIC or the NCUA, so if things crash, the money is gone.

If you choose to join the many people speculating in crypto, just know you could be in for a financial thrill ride. In just a five-year span, the value of a single Bitcoin went from $1,000 up to $20,000, down to $7,000, up to $68,000, and then down to $18,000. So don't put all your eggs into one basket! If you decide to take the risk of investing in crypto, use money you can afford to lose. Dabble in crypto? Cool. Invest all the college money Grandma gave you in Kookycoin? No. Some people found this out the hard way (see next page).

# THE CLOSING BELL

THERE is way more to investing than what we're able to say in this chapter. *Way* more! But hopefully we've inspired you to take the first few steps because investing can be one of the best ways to reach your goal of making $1,000,000.

The big lesson here? It's your money, it's your investment, and it's your responsibility. Taking the time to do your research, not getting in over your head, and making rational decisions are all critical to success. The best part is you're still young and have time to make up for any mistakes. So get investing because time is on your side!

# CRYPTO CAUTIONARY TALE

Crypto is the Wild West of finance, where people have made millions and lost millions.

Think of Laszlo Hanyecz, the unfortunate computer programmer from Florida who paid 10,000 Bitcoin in 2010 for two extra-large pizzas from Papa Johns, to prove that Bitcoin could be used as a medium of exchange. Back then, 10,000 Bitcoin was only worth about $41. That amount of Bitcoin now is worth several hundreds of millions of dollars. Laszlo probably regrets ordering extra-large. May 22 is now known as Bitcoin Pizza Day (true story).

Then there's the famous British YouTuber KSI, who lost over $2.8 million. He had invested heavily in Luna, a very speculative alt coin that plummeted from an all-time high of $119 to basically $0. Like we said earlier, don't be shy to diversify. Throwing your money all in one place is never a good investing strategy, whether it's crypto, Google stock, tulips, or Beanie Babies.

## LONG STORY SHORT

*1. All investments come with risk.*

*2. Do your research.*

*3. ONLY INVEST MONEY YOU CAN AFFORD TO LOSE.*

*4. Diversify to spread the risk.*

# Chapter 11:
# HOW NOT TO BECOME A MILLIONAIRE

**B**Y this time you might be thinking: "What a great book! It's stuffed with all kinds of ways to become rich! All I have to do is follow this advice and I'll have so much cash, I can use it to line my parrot's cage. What could go wrong?"

Well, lots. There are many ways to achieve your financial goals—but there are many more ways to end up with nothing.

Here are the most common ways to blow your dough and keep yourself out of the million-dollar club.

## 1. SPEND MORE THAN YOU EARN.

It seems pretty obvious, but this is the number one reason people don't build up substantial wealth—even people who make a lot of money. A surgeon who carves out $150,000 a month but spends $160,000 will end up worse off than a custodial technician who sweeps up $3,000 a month and socks one-third of it away in the bank.

**The cure:** Make a budget (reread Chapter 3 if you need a refresher). No matter how much money you make, if you don't keep track of what you're spending, you're going to blow it.

## 2. LOAD UP ON DEBT.

Although good for an emergency or an occasional big purchase, credit cards can gobble up your money. If you rely on a credit card, you could end up paying a big interest charge every month if you don't pay off the balance, and that money goes directly in the bank's pocket instead of yours.

**The cure:** Whenever possible, pay cash or use a debit card for your purchases. If you don't have the cash, save up until you have enough to afford it.

## 3. NO PLAN.

People without a financial plan don't know where they are going financially. And without goals it's easy to lose sight of the long-term objective and spend your hard-earned money on something you don't really need, like an 11th pair of jeans.

**The cure:** Make a plan with short-, medium-, and long-term financial goals. Revisit your plan often to make sure it's lining up with your current goals.

## 4. GAMBLE.

For the vast majority of people, gambling means losing. Otherwise, casinos would all go out of business and states would not

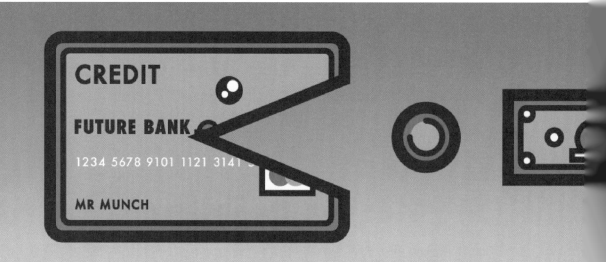

make any money off the lottery. Just remember this simple phrase: "The house always wins in the end."

**The cure:** Don't do it. You'll rarely find a successful millionaire who won their money through gambling. And the vast majority of people who do win the lottery or a gambling jackpot end up blowing it all. There are no shortcuts to a million dollars.

# 5. FALL FOR CONS, SCAMS, FRAUDS & FLIMFLAMS.

Call them what you will, the sad truth is people have thought up a lot of ways to rip you off.

**The cure:** Know your scams—and avoid them. Here are some common ways people will try to separate you from your money.

- **Pyramid scheme:** A "business" model where one person makes money by selling memberships in the business. People who get in early get paid, while others make little or nothing.

- **Ponzi scheme:** Similar to a pyramid scheme, a **Ponzi scheme** gets you to "invest" but pays you with the money others "invested," rather than with money earned by the idea. Only the scammer makes any real money.

- **Phishing:** You might get an email from a company asking you to confirm your account information, your credit card number, or your debit card PIN, or to pay some fee. This is likely a scammer trying to get at your money. No real company will ask for that kind of information by email.

- **Identity theft:** This **fraud** occurs when people steal your personal info so they can

*Loading up on credit card debt will only make your dreams of saving a million evaporate.*

pretend to be you and spend your money. How do they do it? Just a few critical bits of information like your birthday, passwords, or Social Security number can be enough for people to gain access to your accounts. Protect the PIN number on your debit cards, tear up any mail with personal info, don't let mail linger in the mailbox, and safeguard all your personal info.

• **Scholarship scams:** These scams ask for money up front to apply, or tell you they know of "secret" scholarships, or try to get a credit card number. Scholarship information is free and publicly available, and real scholarships never require you to pay.

# WHEN BAD THINGS HAPPEN TO SMART PEOPLE

**W**HAT about the stuff that's out of your hands? Financial misfortune can happen to even the most prepared people. Maybe the transmission in your car unexpectedly blows up.

Maybe your dog suddenly gets sick and you're left with a huge vet bill. Life can be pretty harsh.

What do you do? Expect that bad stuff might happen and prepare for it. That's why experts recommend setting some money aside in a separate emergency fund (at least three to six months' worth of income).

Insurance is another way to protect yourself financially—especially auto, medical, and life insurance. General liability insurance will protect you if you own a business.

*Remember what we said earlier—emergency funds are protection against the angry badgers of life.*

# DOWN BUT NOT OUT

**S**URE, if you want to make a million dollars, it helps to hang on to the money you have. But even if you lose some and find yourself back close to zero, *do not* think that it's all over.

If financial misfortune happens to you, pull yourself back up and get back in the game because that million bucks ain't gonna walk into your pocket all by itself.

# LONG STORY SHORT

1. *Don't spend more than you make.*

2. *Don't load up on debt.*

3. *Don't forget to make a plan with goals.*

4. *Don't gamble.*

5. *Don't fall for a scam.*

# Conclusion:
# GET GOING!

**WELL,** that's our book. We hope you use it as a springboard for ideas on how to make a million dollars. The fact that you're starting early gives you a *huge* advantage.

Just remember to use your newly acquired Million-Dollar Mindset so you don't have to actually save up 1,000,000 individual $1 bills, just enough so that it compounds into $1,000,000. How much is that? Depends on how soon you start saving, how much you save, how much compound interest your investments earn

# WHERE DO MILLIONAIRES GET THEIR MONEY?

According to Brian Tracy, an entrepreneur, author, and professional development trainer, 99% of self-made millionaires come from these four categories:

- **74% started their own business.**

- **10% are folks who climbed the corporate ladder into a senior executive position.**

- **10% are professionals who get paid a lot, such as doctors, lawyers, accountants, and so on.**

- **5% are salespeople and sales consultants who are really good at selling stuff.**

over your lifetime, and how disciplined you can be. We know people who've reached that goal within 10 years. Others are still on their way. Either way, *time is money*. Usually, the longer you let your savings and investments grow, the bigger they get. Keep track of your investments without obsessing over them, and occasionally adjust your plan, goals, budget, and investments to get a little bit better rate of return over the years. If you can keep adding money in baby steps, you'll soon see your savings climbing past the $100,000 mark, then $250,000, $500,000, $800,000, $999,999.99. Don't forget to celebrate when you reach $1,000,000—you've earned it!

## IT'S NEVER TOO LATE

**N**OT everyone can start saving early, but there are lots of ways to make it to $1,000,000.

Let's say you're not able to start saving until you're 30 years old. No problem—it just means you need to get disciplined with saving and seek high returns. Maybe you get a roommate instead of living alone. Maybe you drive a Honda instead of a sportscar. It all starts with the mindset. So even if you start late, you can still make up for lost time with the right mindset. Moral of this story? *Start now!*

# TALK TO A PRO

*Part of being smart about money is knowing when to call in the experts.*

**T**HERE are lots of ways to reach your ultimate goal: finding the right balance among earning, saving, and investing is something you'll have to figure out for yourself. That doesn't mean going it alone. A lot of people will work with a financial adviser to help them manage their money. Many schools offer financial literacy classes, and you can join an investment club. There are a lot of companies that offer free resources. And if you check online, the amount of information is endless.

Still, some of the best (or worst—be careful!) advice can come from family. Some families don't like to talk about money and finances with kids. Others talk about money all the time. We think that talking about money is a good thing, because it helps teach everybody about the family's finances. Maybe you can throw the folks a tip or two about compounding their savings or turn them on to a stock that rakes in the cash.

# KEEP LEARNING

**T**HERE is a lot more cool stuff to discover when it comes to the world of money and finance. The more you learn, the better chance you have at succeeding financially. With a plan, goals, focus, patience, time, resilience, perseverance, quick thinking, and a little luck, you should be able to make it to at least a million dollars. And maybe more . . . so keep learning.

## WE'RE NOT TALKING ABOUT GREED

**W**E need you to stop thinking like a kid for a moment and imagine what your life will be like when you're wrinkled like a prune.

Retirement. Ahhh, the good life: golfing, argyle socks, denture cream, unlimited naps. Unfortunately, a good chunk of Americans are going to spend their "retirement" working—given that 36% of them don't save anything for it. About that same number rely totally on **Social Security** (a government fund that working people are required to pay into, which then provides money to them after they reach a certain age of retirement). Whether or not it's possible to live on Social Security alone, it's not exactly the most fun way to spend your golden years! In fact, the average savings of a 50-year-old American is just $43,797. That won't last very long. And with people living longer (sometimes 30 or more years between the time you retire and the time you expire), that means you'll need a lot more cash to pay for your robotic joints. So don't be a chump with no money left for golf balls. Get into a Million-Dollar Mindset and start putting away money now.

## YOU MADE A MILLION DOLLARS? GREAT. NOW, ZIP IT

**F**LASHING your cash, driving a fancy car, wearing designer shoes, playing the high roller to impress people . . . all that can make you look like a fool. It can also invite friends to expect that you'll pay for everything. Or worse, steal it from you. So when those bucks start rolling in (and if you follow the advice in this book, eventually they will), just zip it. If you are thinking like a millionaire, you'll know to keep a low profile and just be quietly awesome.

*The sooner—and harder—you work, the sooner you can enjoy the rewards.*

# SAVE, SPEND, AND ESPECIALLY SHARE: MILLIONAIRES WHO SPREAD THE WEALTH

Many millionaires make donations to charities and causes they really care about. Giving money to help others is one of the best feelings in the world. Ask any millionaire philanthropist.

## TAYLOR SWIFT

Taylor has been über generous in donating to various causes, big and small! For example:
- $2,000 to a fan for student loans
- $10,000 to a fan battling cancer
- $13,000 to two families behind on rent
- $50,000 to a mom of five kids whose husband died from COVID
- $50,000 to New York City schools
- $70,000 in books to a public library in Pennsylvania
- $250,000 to artist Kesha for legal bills
- $1,000,000 for Nashville tornado relief efforts

## OPRAH WINFREY

Oprah is a billionaire talk show host, actress, and media executive who's donated millions of dollars to some amazing organizations through the Oprah Winfrey Charitable Foundation. She's also provided millions of scholarships to young men, opened a school for young girls in South Africa, become the largest single donor to the Smithsonian museum, and donated over $13 million for COVID relief. Once she even gave everyone in the audience of her daytime talk show $1,000 to donate to the charity of their choice. Now that's called "paying it forward!"

## TONY HAWK

Skateboard legend Tony Hawk, famous for winning over 70 titles and inventing a bunch of slick moves like the Frontside 540-Rodeo Flip, the 900, Ollie-to-Indy, and Gymnast Plant, was the most popular skateboarder of his generation. Today, he has multiple business ventures and his own foundation. With a mission to build safe skateparks in underserved communities, The Skatepark Project has donated over $6 million to build hundreds of skateparks at home and around the world.

# $1,000,000!

**IT** is possible to be poor and happy, or rich and sad, but people who are financially independent have a lot less to worry about than people who are crushed by debt or struggling to pay the bills each month.

Although this book is all about making enough to live a comfortable existence, we hope you realize it's also about enjoying the journey and having fun while you learn to make your million. We also hope you share what you've learned. Maybe by becoming financially independent you're better able to support your community, help lift others out of poverty, and get more kids on the path to financial security. Maybe you'll be so successful, you'll write your own book on how to earn, save, and invest your way to $10 million! And just think, it all started with a goal of saving $100.

Whatever your future, we hope you find financial success and happiness. So get out there and give it your best shot. We'll be here cheering you on while you turn $100 into $1,000,000.

Good luck!

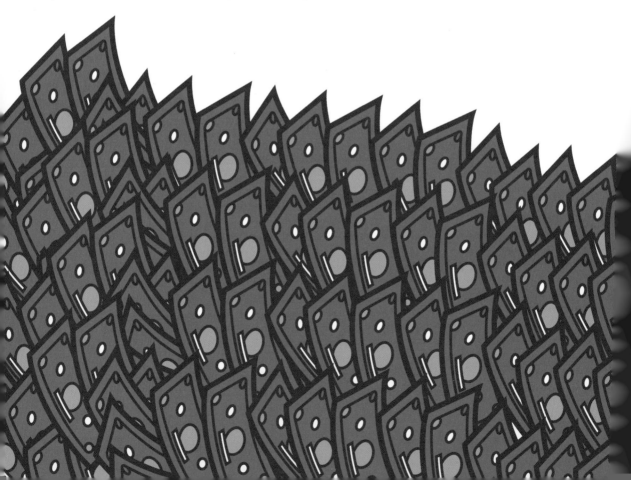

# YOUR PATH TO $1,000,000 CHECKLIST

Go ahead. Take that first step, no matter how small it is, to reach your goal of making a million dollars. Check each box below along the way and track your journey on the next page.

☐ Develop a Million-Dollar Mindset.

☐ Open a savings account at a bank or credit union.

☐ Set financial goals and develop a budget—and stick to them.

☐ Increase your earning power by getting a job or starting a business.

☐ Save up $100, then make regular saving a habit.

☐ Got a few hundred bucks? Move some of your money from your savings account into other investments to maximize interest.

☐ Move some money into an emergency fund. It should equal at least three to six months of your income.

☐ Use the power of time and compound interest to really grow, grow, grow your bucks.

☐ Avoid all the dumb things people do to lose money once they have it.

☐ Go play golf (or Ultimate Frisbee) like a millionaire.

# READY? SET? GO!

DISCOVER YOUR MILLION-DOLLAR MINDSET

GO GET $100!

ODD JOBS

ALLOWANCE

BIRTHDAY

EXTRA CHORES

FIRED!

BADGER BITE!

STOCKS RISE!

PROMOTION!

STOCKS FALL!

1

5

4

3

GOT $100? YES?—GO FORWARD! NO?—GO BACK!

OPEN A SAVINGS ACCOUNT

SET UP A BUDGET!

DON'T FORGET TO SET UP AN EMERGENCY FUND!

# YOUR TWO-PAGE
# PLAN TO BECOME A
# MILLIONAIRE

NAME: _____

AGE: _____

GOAL: _____ **$1,000,000!**

_____

_____

## COMMITMENT STATEMENT

Add your current age to the number of years you think it will take to become a millionaire. Look at yourself in the mirror and repeat this statement:

"I, _____,
WILL BECOME A MILLIONAIRE BY THE TIME
I AM _____ YEARS OLD."

(Be realistic. Give yourself enough time and modify as you go along.)

## SETTING FINANCIAL GOALS

List your short-, medium-, and long-term goals. (Your long-term goal should be $1,000,000 or more.)

Short-term goal (less than 1 year):
$_____

Medium-term goal (1 to 10 years):
$_____

Long-term goal (10+ years):
$_____

# EARNING INCOME

List all the ways you'll get money to achieve your goals:

Allowance: _____

_____

Work/Job: _____

_____

Extra Jobs: _____

_____

Start a Business: _____

_____

Interest on Investments: _____

_____

Gifts/Inheritance: _____

_____

# KEEPING A BUDGET

Create a budget that will help you achieve your financial goals (and don't forget to set up a savings account!):

MONTHLY INCOME: $_____
MONTHLY EXPENSES: $_____
Savings (Pay Yourself First): $_____
Transportation: $_____
Phone bill: $_____
Media downloads: $_____
School supplies: $_____
Food: $_____
Clothes: $_____
Entertainment: $_____
Other: $_____
Total: $_____
If your expenses total more than your income, you'll blow your budget. Revise!

# CHECKING IN AND REVISING

Check your progress with your goals—do it yearly, monthly, or weekly. How are you doing? Do you need to revise anything?

_____

Who can help you with this? Be your mentor? Hold you accountable?

_____

How often will you check in with them? _____

# YOUR ONE-PAGE BUSINESS PLAN

## BUSINESS NAME

_____

## THE "BIG IDEA"

_____
_____
_____

## MARKETING MADNESS

**PRODUCT:** What are you selling and who will buy it? _____

**PRICE:** How much will you charge for your product or service? _____

**PLACE:** Where can people buy your product or service? _____

**PROMOTION:** How will you get the word out? _____

## MAKE A PROFIT

Calculate your profit potential for a one-month period.

**TOTAL INCOME:** _____
**TOTAL EXPENSES:** _____
**PROFIT (INCOME MINUS EXPENSES):** _____

Making a profit? Great! You're off to a good start. If not, go back and see if you can increase your income or decrease your expenses. What's next? Make sure you hand out your plan to family, friends, and potential investors!

## DRAW YOUR BUSINESS LOGO

# YOUR PERSONAL BUDGET TRACKER

Here's a simple budget tracker to help you get started. Photocopy it five times, and you've got yourself a one-month budget to play with. Each day enter any income earned and expenses owed.

## ---DAY 1---

### INCOME

| Item | Amount |
|------|--------|
| _____ | _____ |
| _____ | _____ |
| _____ | _____ |

Total: _____

### EXPENSES

| Item | Amount |
|------|--------|
| _____ | _____ |
| _____ | _____ |
| _____ | _____ |
| _____ | _____ |
| _____ | _____ |

Total: _____

## ---DAY 2---

### INCOME

| Item | Amount |
|------|--------|
| _____ | _____ |
| _____ | _____ |
| _____ | _____ |

Total: _____

### EXPENSES

| Item | Amount |
|------|--------|
| _____ | _____ |
| _____ | _____ |
| _____ | _____ |
| _____ | _____ |
| _____ | _____ |

Total: _____

## ---DAY 3---

### INCOME

| Item | Amount |
|------|--------|
| _____ | _____ |
| _____ | _____ |
| _____ | _____ |

Total: _____

### EXPENSES

| Item | Amount |
|------|--------|
| _____ | _____ |
| _____ | _____ |
| _____ | _____ |
| _____ | _____ |
| _____ | _____ |

Total: _____

## ---DAY 4---

### INCOME

| Item | Amount |
|------|--------|
| _____ | _____ |
| _____ | _____ |

Total: _____

### EXPENSES

| Item | Amount |
|------|--------|
| _____ | _____ |
| _____ | _____ |
| _____ | _____ |
| _____ | _____ |

Total: _____

# ---DAY 5---

## INCOME

Item                          Amount

_____|_____
_____|_____
_____|_____
         Total: _____

## EXPENSES

Item                          Amount

_____|_____
_____|_____
_____|_____
_____|_____
         Total: _____

# ---DAY 6---

## INCOME

Item                          Amount

_____|_____
_____|_____
_____|_____
         Total: _____

## EXPENSES

Item                          Amount

_____|_____
_____|_____
_____|_____
_____|_____
         Total: _____

# ---DAY 7---

## INCOME

Item                          Amount

_____|_____
_____|_____
_____|_____
         Total: _____

## EXPENSES

Item                          Amount

_____|_____
_____|_____
_____|_____
         Total: _____

# ---DAY 8---

## INCOME

Item | Amount
_____|_____
_____|_____
_____|_____

Total: _____

## EXPENSES

Item | Amount
_____|_____
_____|_____
_____|_____
_____|_____
_____|_____

Total: _____

# ---DAY 9---

## INCOME

Item | Amount
_____|_____
_____|_____
_____|_____

Total: _____

## EXPENSES

Item | Amount
_____|_____
_____|_____
_____|_____
_____|_____
_____|_____

Total: _____

# ---DAY 10---

## INCOME

Item | Amount
_____|_____
_____|_____
_____|_____

Total: _____

## EXPENSES

Item | Amount
_____|_____
_____|_____
_____|_____
_____|_____
_____|_____

Total: _____

# ---DAY 11---

## INCOME

Item | Amount
_____|_____
_____|_____
_____|_____

Total: _____

## EXPENSES

Item | Amount
_____|_____
_____|_____
_____|_____
_____|_____
_____|_____

Total: _____

## ---DAY 12---

### INCOME

Item                    Amount

_____|_____
_____|_____
_____|_____

Total: _____

### EXPENSES

Item                    Amount

_____|_____
_____|_____
_____|_____
_____|_____
_____|_____

Total: _____

## ---DAY 13---

### INCOME

Item                    Amount

_____|_____
_____|_____
_____|_____

Total: _____

### EXPENSES

Item                    Amount

_____|_____
_____|_____
_____|_____
_____|_____
_____|_____

Total: _____

## ---DAY 14---

### INCOME

Item                    Amount

_____|_____
_____|_____
_____|_____

Total: _____

### EXPENSES

Item                    Amount

_____|_____
_____|_____
_____|_____
_____|_____
_____|_____

Total: _____

# Glossary

**BANK** a business that keeps money for individual people or companies, exchanges currencies, makes loans, and offers other financial services

**BOND** a debt instrument issued by a government or company promising to pay back borrowed money at a fixed rate of interest on a specified date

**BORROWER** a person who gets money for a period of time knowing that the money must be returned

**BROKER** a specially licensed person who trades stocks on the exchanges for other people

**BUDGET** a plan specifying how resources, especially time or money, will be allocated or spent during a particular period

**BULL OR BEAR MARKET** A bull market is a period of generally rising prices. A bear market is a general decline in the stock market over a period of time.

**BUSINESS PLAN** a plan that sets out the future strategy and financial development of a business, usually covering a period of several years

**BUY LOW AND SELL HIGH** When buying and selling stock in particular, it's best to purchase when the cost is low and then sell when the price is high, thus increasing your profit (much easier said than done).

**CAREER** a job or occupation regarded as a long-term or lifelong activity

**CD (CERTIFICATE OF DEPOSIT)** similar to a savings account in that it is insured and thus virtually risk-free, though it requires a deposit for a set period of time

**COMMISSION** a fee paid to an agent for providing a service, especially a percentage of the total amount of business transacted

**COMPOUND INTEREST** interest calculated on the initial principal and also on the accumulated interest of previous periods of a deposit or loan

**COVID PANDEMIC OF 2020** a deadly pandemic that caused the worst economic downturn since the Great Depression

**CREDIT** a loan of money between a borrower and a lender. The debt is then repaid through a series of payments, plus interest. A credit card is a classic example.

**CREDIT UNION** a cooperative savings association that offers financial services to its members at reduced interest rates

**CROWDFUNDING** the practice of raising funds from a large group of people (usually) over the Internet toward a common service, project, product, investment, cause, or experience

**CUSTODIAL ACCOUNT** an account managed by somebody other than the person who benefits from it, e.g., by a parent for a child

**DEBT** an amount of money, a service, or an item of property that is owed to somebody

**DIRECT DEPOSIT** a paycheck electronically deposited into your bank account

**DIVERSIFICATION** reducing your risk by having a variety of investments. We can't explain it any better than "Don't put all your eggs in one basket."

**DIVIDEND** stockholders' share of a company's profit, paid either in cash or more shares

**ECONOMIC DOWNTURN** a drop or reduction in the success of a business or economy

**EMERGENCY FUND** money saved for unexpected expenses, such as having to replace the phone you dropped in the toilet

**EXCHANGE** where the trading of commodities, securities, or other assets takes place

**EXPENSES** the amount of money spent in order to buy or do something

**FINANCIAL FREEDOM** having enough money to live comfortably without actively working, if you don't want to. What that amount may be is up to you. For some, it is more than a million dollars. For others, it is less than a million dollars.

**FRAUD** the crime of obtaining money or some other benefit by deliberate deception

**GREAT DEPRESSION OF THE 1930s** the deepest and longest economic downturn in U.S. history, which started with the Stock Market Crash of October 1929

**GREAT RECESSION OF 2008** an economic downturn that began in December 2007, when 8.4 million people lost their jobs in the U.S.

**INCOME** the amount of money received over a period of time as payment for work, goods, services, or investments

**INDEX** the average price of a chosen group of stocks traded on an exchange like the NYSE or NASDAQ

**INDEX FUND** a mutual fund that invests in companies listed in an important stock market index in order to match the market's overall performance

**INHERITANCE** something, often money or goods, passed on when a person dies

**INTEREST** a small fee that a borrower pays to a lender. Or, the money a bank pays for principal you have in an account.

**INTERNSHIP** a method of on-the-job training

**INVEST** to put money into a business, project, property, and so on, with the plan of making more money

**LENDER** a person or institution that offers money with the understanding it will be returned

**LISTED** describes a company that has been listed on a stock market exchange so people can buy/sell shares in it

**LOAN** when one person borrows money from another. This debt is repaid by the borrower to the lender, usually with interest.

**LONG-TERM GOAL** a plan ranging over at least 10 years

**LOSS** when you sell off your investment and lose money (boo)

**MARKET CAPITALIZATION** the stock price of a publicly traded company multiplied by all the shares owned

**MARKETING** the process of communicating the value of a product or service to customers

**MEDIUM-TERM GOAL** a plan of action completed in fewer than 10 years

**MUTUAL FUND** a collection of investments, purchased by money collected from many investors. Mutual funds are generally not insured like a savings account. They are an investment tool, usually managed by a fund manager, so check for fees and know the success history of the fund before you invest.

**PAY YOURSELF FIRST (PYF)** just like it sounds—put money into your savings before you start paying bills, spending it, or giving it away

**P/E RATIO** the relationship between the stock price and the company's earnings (profit) per share of stock

**PONZI SCHEME** a pyramid investment swindle, named after Charles Ponzi (1882–1949), in which supposed "profits" are paid to early investors from money actually invested by later participants. Ponzi was a businessman and con artist who became known in the early 1920s as a swindler for his moneymaking scheme.

**PORTFOLIO** the group of stocks, bonds, real estate, or anything else you have invested your money in

**PRINCIPAL** here we mean the money you start with, not the person whom you get sent to when you act out in class

**PRIVATE VS. PUBLIC COMPANY** a privately owned company is owned by private investors, shareholders, or owners; there is no way you can invest in one. A publicly owned company offers its securities (stock/shares, bonds/loans, etc.) for sale.

**PRODUCT** the material sold as finished goods, also known as a commodity

**PROFIT** what's left over when you subtract expenses from revenues

**PROFIT POTENTIAL** how much money you can really make (a little more specific than "The sky's the limit")

**PROSPECTUS** a legal document that has all the information about a business that someone might want to invest in

**RATE OF RETURN** a profit on an investment over a period of time, expressed as a percentage of the original investment

**RATING AGENCY** a company that issues credit ratings for the debt of public and private corporations

**RECORD** a music disc made of vinyl that would sometimes break and play the same thing over and over and over and over and over and over

**REFERENCE** a statement concerning somebody's (your) character or qualifications from someone you know or have worked for

**RÉSUMÉ** a written description of your work experience and education, usually on one page

**RETIREMENT** when you've done everything in this book, made your million dollars, and no longer need to work for a living

**RISK AND REWARD** offsetting the chance of something going bad (risk) with the hope something will be very good (reward)

**RULE OF 72** a simple method for roughly determining how long it will take for an investment to double in value at a specific rate of interest

**SAVINGS ACCOUNT** a bank account that earns interest on money deposited

**SERVICE** a set of actions performed to benefit your customers

**SHARE** a way of measuring ownership of something. For example, you might own a "share" of a company by purchasing it on the stock market. You can own one share, or millions of shares, in one investment, or many.

**SHORT-TERM GOAL** an immediate plan of action

**SIMPLE INTEREST** a quick way to calculate the cost of interest only on the principal of a loan

**SOCIAL SECURITY** a social insurance program run by the federal government that gives out retirement, disability, and survivors' benefits

**STATE LABOR LAWS** rules in each state that protect the rights and state the duties of workers and employers

**STOCK** a share in the capital of a company or a unit of ownership (specifically, "common stock")

**STOCK MARKET** a market where securities are bought and sold

**STOCK SPLIT** the division of shares of stock so that shareholders receive more shares at a proportionately lower value, leaving the total value unchanged

**TARGET MARKET** the specific customers that a company wants to sell its products or services to

**UNDERVALUE** to judge the value (worth) of a company as being lower than it really is (or how you may feel after you've done all your chores and no one says thank you)

**VALUE INVESTING** investment in stocks believed to be worth far more than their current prices

**WALL STREET** a street in New York City that runs through the historical center of the Financial District, which contains the headquarters of many of the city's major financial institutions. It's also the home of the world's largest stock exchange, the New York Stock Exchange, and a figure of speech for all the financial markets of the United States as a whole.

**WINDFALL** a significant, unexpected, large amount of money received at one time

# ABOUT THE AUTHORS

James McKenna and Jeannine Glista, along with Erren Gottlieb, are co-creators of Biz Kid$, a financial education initiative based on the Emmy Award–winning, nationally syndicated public TV series of the same name. James and Erren live and save their money in Seattle, WA. Jeannine lives and saves her money in Sacramento, CA.

Matt Fontaine is a writer who lives and saves his money on Vashon Island, WA. You can find him at thinksmartmouth.com.

The *Biz Kid$* series has been seen by more than 20 million people since its premiere in 2008. It is broadcast worldwide and accessible through numerous outlets. The series is cocreated and co-executive-produced by the creators of *Bill Nye the Science Guy*. It has also been approved as a financial education recommended resource in 16 states. *Biz Kid$* is complemented by a resource-rich website with free lesson plans, online games, and community activities at bizkids.com.